CONCILIUM

FELIX WILFRED

Felix Wilfred, a long time member of the *Concilium* editorial board and editor of many issues, was elected the new president of *Concilium* at the Annual Meeting held in Münster in June 2007.

Felix Wilfred once told us how he managed to speak twelve languages: 'I study a little grammar of the language I like to learn, and then I start reading the New Testament in this language. I know the stories – and I keep reading until I know the language.'

In many other aspects, he is likewise extraordinary. He is a person who crosses borders and redefines borders as he crosses them. He has lectured and taught all over the word, combining the fields of sociology, history, anthropology, philosophy, and religious studies, as well as combining hermeneutical reflections with socio-political siding with those who live, worldwide, at the margins.

– *The Editors*

CONCILIUM 2008/1

HOMOSEXUALITIES

Edited by
Marcella Althaus-Reid, Regina Ammicht Quinn,
Erik Borgman, Norbert Reck

SCM Press · London

Published by SCM Press, 13–17 Long Lane, London EC1A 9PN

Copyright © International Association of Conciliar Theology, Madras (India)

English translations copyright © 2008 SCM-Canterbury Press Ltd

All rights reserved. No part of this publication may be
reproduced, stored in a retrieval system, or transmitted,
in any form or by any means, electronic, mechanical, photocopying,
recording or otherwise, without the written prior permission of
Concilium, Asian Centre for Cross-Cultural Studies, 40/6A Panayur Kuppan Road,
Sholinganallur Post, Panayur, Madras 60099, India.

ISBN 978 0 334 03097 3

Printed in the UK by CPI William Clowes Ltd,
Beccles, NR34 7TL

Concilium published February, April, June, October
December

Contents

I. Homosexualities

'We' and 'Others': In Place of an Introduction
REGINA AMMICHT QUINN   9

Dangerous Desires: Catholic Approaches to Same-sex Sexuality
NORBERT RECK   15

Sexual Identity, Culture, Politics: Evaluations

(A) The Moral Values of Europe: Marks or Wounds of Civilization?
JULIE CLAGUE   29

(B) Homosexuality in South Africa
CHARLES RYAN   39

(C) 'The Silent War': How Latin American Women can be What They Want
NANCY CARDOSO PEREIRA   49

(D) 'A G-string is not Samoan': Exploring a Transgressive Third-Gender Pasifika Theology
PHILIP CULBERTSON AND TAVITA MALIKO   62

Unfixing Nature: Homosexuality and Innovating Natural Law
ERIC BORGMAN   73

On Queer Theology and Liberation Theology: The Irruption of the Sexual Subject in Theology
MARCELLA ALTHAUS-REID   83

Encountering Beasts: Lesbian Biblical Hermeneutics on the Road
  DERYN GUEST   97

Letter to a Young Gay Catholic
  JAMES ALISON   109

II. Theological Forum

Reading the Signs of the Times: *Concilium*, Partner in a
Common Journey
  FELIX WILFRED   121

Humanae Vitae: A Global Reassessment after Forty Years

(A) Considerations beyond the Birth-Control Controversy
  DIETMAR MIETH   125

(B) Challenges of Updating *Humanae Vitae*
  MÁRCIO FABRI DOS ANJOS   131

(C) A Philippine Assessment
  JOSÉ DE MESA   138

Committed Love and Relational Justice
  MARY E. HUNT   145

Contributors   151

I. HOMOSEXUALITIES

'We' and 'Others': In Place of an Introduction

Identities

Problems of identity are questions of our time that fundamentally concern our personal, social, and overall existence. In personal life, identities are often no longer simply given but have to be chosen and discovered. In general political life, the forging of a common identity can act as the basis of belonging and consequently become the starting-point for protest against discrimination and contempt directed against a specific group of people: 'We' are blacks, miners, women, and so on, and 'we blacks', 'we miners', 'we women', and so on fight for our rights. At the same time an emphasis on identity can form the basis of divisions, enmities, expulsions, and war: 'We' come from this town, or this tribe, and belong to this religion, and define the 'others' as 'them' and different from us.

Felix Wilfred, who introduces himself as the new President of *Concilium* in this issue, calls questions of identity in all their ambivalence signs of the present times. They may be life-promoting, but they can also become symptoms of disease and constitute the 'syndrome of singular identity' (Wilfred).

'Identities are robustly plural' says the Indian Nobel Prize-winner Amartya Sen:[1]

> The same person can be, without any contradiction, an American citizen, of Caribbean origin, with African ancestry, a Christian, a liberal, a woman, a vegetarian, a long-distance runner, a historian, a schoolteacher, a novelist, a feminist, a heterosexual, a believer in gay and lesbian rights, a theatre lover. . . . Each of these collectives, to all of which this person simultaneously belongs, gives her a particular identity. None of them can be taken to be the person's only identity or singular membership category.[2]

If people are reduced to a single identity, the result is a system of classifications – according to religion or culture or nation or race or sexual preference. These classifications have power over people. They reduce and devalue people and exert violence through this very devaluation:

> The art of constructing hatred takes the form of invoking the magical power of some allegedly predominant identity that drowns other affiliations, and in a convenient bellicose form can also overpower any human sympathy or natural kindness that we may normally have. . . . In fact, a major source of potential conflict in the contemporary world is the presumption that people can be uniquely categorized based on religion or culture. The implicit belief in the overarching power of a singular classification can make the world thoroughly inflammable.[3]

Homosexualities

The theme of this issue is 'homosexualities' – a topic to be considered in a 'robust plural' form, and one that encompasses a wide range of ways of seeing oneself and ways of life. 'Homosexualities' (especially in the western notion of them as affected by Christianity) are an aspect of the composition of many strata of identity. The way in which people with a sexual preference for persons of their own gender are seen often combines desire and disdain. It both craves and devalues because sexual activity between members of the same sex is equated with excessive and inconsequential pleasure, which is simultaneously viewed with envy and contempt. This attitude identifies such individuals in terms of their sexuality (or, more exactly, in terms of their partner's sexual organs), whereas heterosexual people are represented by means of a wide range of characteristics and situations: by race and class, abilities and profession, nationality and geography, status, and so forth. Any singular identification of this kind is a form of violence.

We must remember that 'homosexuality' understood as a singular disposition determining one's identity is a historically new and not a 'globalized' concept. Whether in the history of Christianity or in Samoa the appearance of people of the same gender as sexual partners or loving couples is a constant feature of human history that has produced a wide range of forms, interpretations, and value-judgments.

Conflicts regarding homosexuality generally conform to three basic patterns. The first is a lack or rejection of fertility; in this respect (and not only in the sexual policy of Nazi Germany), homosexuality and abortion are treated in the same context.[4] The second basic pattern is the identification of 'sodomites' or 'homosexuals' with sexual excess, or sheer lust, which others find unattainable, secretly desirable, and dangerous. The third basic pattern is the disturbance of a hierarchical order viewed as natural. In the context of classical antiquity (Philo is an appropriate example in this regard), sexual acts are not morally 'right' or 'wrong' because of the gender of the particular partner. Other factors are more important, such as avoiding excess and, especially, the question of hierarchy in the sense of deciding who plays the active and who the passive role. The passive role was acceptable for 'naturally' inferior persons – women, slaves, or young people who were not yet citizens. Therefore sexual acts between free adult males became problematical.

Accordingly women are initially invisible in these concepts of homosexuality, while the concepts themselves rely on a misogynistic logic and operate as a form of defence against the 'feminine' in the male self-understanding and understanding of others.

The decisive approach here is the question of the 'normality' of heterosexuality, to which all three basic patterns of conflict in post-modern forms of existence – the rejection of fertility, 'inconsequential' sexual intercourse, and the disturbance of a hierarchical order viewed as natural – can appear the same.

Therefore the theme of this issue is 'homosexualities', in order to provide a starting-point for proficient reconsideration of traditional patterns of thought.

Homosexualities and the Church

Christianity has repeatedly conceived 'homosexuality' as sinful. The background to this viewpoint is the conception of heterosexual marriage based on natural law, which sees sex in marriage as justified by fertility. In certain Christian contexts 'homosexuality' would seem to be the phenomenon that Christian morality uses in an attempt at self-definition. Then whatever 'homosexuality' prevents or averts is seen as 'Christian' – in a world of wars and ethnic cleansing, famine and injustice. This equation of Christian morality with a condemnation of homosexuality is usually justified by reference to 'irregular' use of sexual organs.

A first step beyond this is taken when – as in the *Catechism of the Catholic Church* – we are told that it is wrong to subject homosexuals to 'unjust discrimination' (No. 2358). Even though the phraseology would seem to suggest that there is just and unjust discrimination of human beings, this statement is a major advance. But it is a step in the wrong direction. It is a step towards the establishment or reinforcement of a divisive category.

The Catechism tells us that 'the homosexual' should be treated respectfully, sympathetically, and tactfully. Sympathy and tact are often attitudes to people who suffer from a serious deficiency, or whose human existence itself is defined as deficient. Therefore the recommendation that 'such' people should be treated with 'respect' would seem to be a rhetorical device that both calls for respect yet relies on an essential contempt. It consolidates a form of being 'other' that is classed as morally deficient, and allows for the separation of 'abnormal' people from 'us'.

'A spiritual decolonization'

Amartya Sen sees the way out of the impasse of singular identities as demanding a 'spiritual decolonization'.

A colonized mind and spirit affects both sides: the dominant and the dominated. One's own identity is always defined in separation from 'the other': whether I claim a dominant normality for myself, or I accept for myself the ascription of a devalued status by a majority even to the point of inability to survive or suicide; or I radically reverse the dominant valuation and judge that 'other' to be quite worthless. All these are violent attempts to establish singular identities and classifications.

A 'spiritual decolonization' means abandoning simplistic classifications. This process must have political, economic, social, and religious consequences – in a world that remains divided into 'us' and 'them'.

We hope that this issue on 'homosexualities' will initiate a 'spiritual decolonization'. We are aware that among Christian Churches, and especially in the Catholic Church, this is a difficult theme. In Christian circles 'homosexuality' has an imprecisely defined yet clearly presented tradition. It often appears as a topic of sexual morals in various forms of discourse about sin, and it is fundamentally associated with anxiety. It is a theme that has long been treated to date in a 'colonized' way with the aid of precise classifications, moral condemnations, and singular identities.

A 'decolonized' mode of perceiving, thinking, and talking about homosexualities is not intended to represent a 'minority', a group of people who are 'other', and to whom 'normal' people ought to be 'nice'. It is not primarily a matter of changing one's valuation of the category of 'homosexual-

'We' and 'Others': In Place of an Introduction 13

ity' (from 'bad' to 'not so bad', from 'disgusting' to 'actually quite nice'). Instead the questions we have to ask are: What value do we place on classifications of this kind? What are the probable reasons for using them? What is the part played by the Christian religion in problems of categorization and possibilities of breaking away from these classifications?

It is irregular 'queer studies', an approach capable of surmounting boundaries and dissolving categorizations, that can discern and reflect on the rich variety of thought and of the life of *all human beings*.

Accordingly, our consideration of 'homosexualities' is neither an examination by moral philosophers of appropriate sexual activities nor a disquisition by liberal theologians on 'others'. It is a consideration by humans of humans, their relationships, their desires, their pleasure, and their sharing in and their contribution to human existence in all its rich complexity. It is a consideration by humans of humans, and a consideration of a specific form of desire that is unequivocally more hazardous than same-sex desire: the wish to stereotype 'others' with a singular and simultaneously devalued identity and thereby to make it possible for violence to prevail.

Our thanks go to Maria Clara Bingemer, Diego Irrarázaval, Mary Hunt, Dennis Gira and Edward Farrugia for their suggestions. We should also like to thank Pramila Rajan in Madras for her support, and Elaine Wainwright, who made it possible for us to consider Oceania.

Concilium begins its 'Theological Forum' with this issue, thus providing space in each number for up-to-date discussions, 'signs of the times', and other interesting texts. We hope that you will find these contributions of value.

On behalf of the editors:
Regina Ammicht Quinn

Translated by J. G. Cumming

Notes

1. Amartya Sen, *Identity and Violence*, New York & London, 2006, p.19.
2. *Ibid.*, xiii.
3. *Ibid.*, xv.
4. In October 1936 Heinrich Himmler established the 'National Central Office for Action against Homosexuality and Abortion'. It was devoted to the 'central

surveys' and 'effective eradication' of these two 'national plagues'. From 1940, after their release from imprisonment, homosexuals sentenced in accordance with Paragraph 175 of the Criminal Code 'who had seduced more than one partner' were despatched to concentration camps. At the same time, the measure known as 'protective custody' was used against increasingly larger circles of homosexual men and also lesbians. The groups of people who counted as 'communally unacceptable' were 'persons whose immoral conduct excludes them from the racial community. . . . They include streetwalkers, pimps, sexual offenders, homosexuals and so on.' Cf. Burkhard Jellonnek, *Homosexuelle unterm Hakenkreuz*, Paderborn, 1990, pp. 134–9; Claudia Schoppmann, *Nationalsozialistische Sexualpolitik und weibliche Homosexualität*, Pfaffenweiler, 1991, pp. 208–14.

Dangerous Desires: Catholic Approaches to Same-sex Sexuality

NORBERT RECK

The Catholic Church's attitude to homosexuality is said to be consistent and to have been intransigent throughout the centuries. Close examination of these assumptions shows that neither of them is true. An official position of the whole Church in this respect was arrived at only after hundreds of years; the types of argument advanced to support it varied considerably; and the concept of 'homosexuality' characteristic of our present-day view of same-sex sexual activities has existed only since the late 1860s. In order to avoid generalizations and misinterpretations, it is best to beware of applying modern notions to very different periods of human history. In general, the opinions of same-sex desire proffered in the course of Christian history do not accord with the ideas of our own times.

Since space is limited, I shall restrict myself to an attempt to shed light on certain salient points in this history. First of all, it is essential to clarify what is understood by 'same-sex desire' before tackling theological standpoints and church documents in this regard.

I. The phenomenon of same-sex desire

Men and women who have felt drawn to persons of the same sex have existed at all times and in all cultures. This universal reality justifies the claim that longing between persons of the same sex is a constant of human history. There is no evidence to support the hypothesis that same-sex desire occurs only as a symptom of decadence in societies in decline. The art and literature of all epochs feature the sexual and friendly relations, adventures, and love stories of people of the same sex. These portrayals originate in societies of all kinds and stages of development, both prosperous and declining. For instance, the Gilgamesh epic of Mesopotamia (the earliest complete version has been dated to about 1700 BC) tells us that the mythical King Gilgamesh fell in love with the savage Enkidu 'as with a spouse'. In the *Iliad*, Homer describes the friendship of Achilles and Patroclus in the twelfth century BC. The Hebrew Bible contains David's poem of lamentation over Jonathan, whose love for him was 'wonderful, passing the love of women' (2 Sam. 1.26).[1] In the sixth century BC, the Greek poet Sappho celebrated ardent love between women in verses that still touch the heart. From the third century BC, at the time of Confucius, we have an account of the friendship between Duke Ling and his favourite Mizi Xia: 'When passing through an orchard, the young man offered to share his peach with his friend, instead of eating it on his own, and thus the "love of a shared peach" became an expression for homosexual affection for many centuries.'[2] In the epic *Mahabharata*, which originated in India around 200 BC, the friendship between Krishna and Arjuna is described as a force that rendered both of them immortal.

We know of societies that reject relationships of this kind, and of others that prize and promote them. Of course, we cannot properly make general statements about the forms in which people live out their same-sex desire, or about how they see themselves in that situation. Whereas some people think they are doing something forbidden, others take same-sex activities for granted; some people are interested only in members of the same sex, whereas others enjoy sexual relations with men and women; and for some individuals sex is to the fore, whereas for others their desire turns on an intimate friendship. Among the Samurai of sixteenth- to eighteenth-century Japan the love of adult men for youths was the rule: 'The future Samurai is loved by adult men until he comes of age, then he loves youths who are younger than him, and finally, a few years later, he sets up a household with a woman.'[3] In some Papuan tribes of New Guinea all boys live together from childhood until they become adults, and pre-pubertal boys pleasure the adolescents orally in the course of something like institutionalized fellatio. After this period, young men usually begin relationships with women and marry them.[4]

Objections that these examples might be said to have nothing to do with homosexuality are quite correct. They are instances of very different sexual and friendly activities between people of the same sex, but do not illustrate the notion of a constitutionally conditioned, identity-constitutive homosexuality that has become a general feature of western industrial nations in the modern era. To be sure, the contrary conclusion is not automatically the case. If a historical personage is not to be characterized as 'homosexual', that does not mean that he or she is necessarily to be described as 'heterosexual.' For instance, the question whether King David or Alexander the Great was homosexual or heterosexual is meaningless. Neither of them knew of any such categories; they did not entertain or express their feelings in accordance with them; and they did not live in ways definable by the boundaries of these terms. Their experience was determined by quite different categories and guidelines.

Clearly the modern dichotomy of heterosexuality and homosexuality does not characterize the spectrum of human sexual behaviour-patterns proficiently. This is also true of the contemporary world, and of western societies in which in a majority of cases nowadays gender relations are construed in accordance with this dichotomy. The Kinsey Reports[5] published in the USA halfway through the twentieth century showed that in each case the behaviour of precisely 5 percent of the subjects investigated for the surveys was unequivocally and exclusively homosexual or heterosexual. No unequivocal allocation was possible for the remaining 90 percent. Accordingly, the divisions of the scale of sexual behaviours arrived at by Alfred Kinsey are fluid, and most sexual behaviour falls into a mixed area. He concluded that not everything was black or white, that the world could not be divided into sheep and goats, and that it was a taxonomic principle that nature seldom featured separate categories: 'Males do not represent two discrete populations, heterosexual and homosexual. . . . Only the human mind invents categories and tries to force facts into pigeonholes. The living world is a continuum in each and every one of its aspects.'[6] He was convinced that a proficient understanding of reality depended on awareness of this truth as applied to human sexual behaviour

His observations persuaded Kinsey that the characterization of people as 'homosexuals' had to be discarded in principle. At the most one might speak of individuals with a specific amount of heterosexual experience and a specific amount of homosexual experience.[7]

Similarly, in his *Three Treatises on Sexual Theory*, Freud had already confirmed the fact that sexual feelings between people of the same sex were certainly not restricted to a small group of persons to be differentiated from the mass on the grounds of morally or psychopathologically distinct characteristics:

> Psychoanalytical research is quite decisively opposed to any attempt to separate homosexuals from other people as a group with an altogether

different disposition. On studying forms of sexual arousal other than those that are manifestly advertised, it discovers that all humans are capable of choosing persons of the same sex as objects of desire and have also done so in the unconscious.[8]

At all events, this daring confirmation on the basis of his own research must have been as unsettling for Freud as it assuredly was for most of his contemporaries. If erotic or sexual feelings for people of the same sex were actually something known to *all* people to some extent, then those *feelings were dangerous*. They were capable of calling in question not only traditional gender arrangements, but identity patterns that had come to be taken for granted, as well as the demarcation-lines of socio-cultural institutions and attitudes. Freud thought that this danger might be evaded by ascribing the same-sex feelings found in all individuals to a specific phase of human development. Such feelings had their place in the course of development, but at some point they had to be sublimated in social activities, until a human being finally matured to the point of choosing the 'correct' sexual object.

Freud never happened upon the proof that same-sex desire was 'normal' in a certain stage of human development and sick outside this phase. He merely posited it in accordance with the principle that what may not be cannot be. The fact that desire of this kind occurred even in appropriately living, healthy people of all ages and classes leading appropriate lives would necessarily have led to his thesis collapsing already. But Freud was determined to retain his Oedipal model of human development, and he declared that all those who maintained same-sex desires beyond a specific point in childhood, and did not wish to sublimate them, were neurotic and paranoid.[9]

We cannot know what is truly 'normal' or even 'natural' in these matters. We are all so profoundly marked by our own culture, by what is taken to be 'normal' in this culture, that we can never say with absolute assurance who we are 'by nature' and what we would feel 'in a natural state'. Long before we develop a desire for sexual contacts, most of us have parents who act as our role models, we have listened to fairy tales in which Cinderella eventually marries the handsome prince, and we have seen countless films in which the 'happy ending' always turns out to be the marriage of a man and a woman. Moreover, in many contemporary cultures same-sex feelings are bound up with shame and anxiety, so that it is difficult actually to attend and yield to all our own wishes and longings. What an important study by the theologian Isolde Karle says about the body and its reactions also applies to human sexual desires. Desire certainly exists in a pre-social state but can only be read culturally, and then transformed socially.[10]

Consequently we cannot say what sexual desire was like 'before any culture' or 'at the beginning'. Nevertheless, I think that Guy Hocquenghem's inclusivist viewpoint, which accepts homosexual desire, but not the division of humankind into 'homosexuals' and 'heterosexuals', has hit upon something vital here: 'At the beginning desire is a universally widespread whole, a unity consisting of various non-exclusive tendencies, of forms of eroticism and so forth combined on an "and–and" and not on an "either–or" basis'.[11]

In the course of history, this whole comprising different tendencies or ways of seeking to be physically and mentally close to others is fragmented in some cultures. Some of these fragments are taken to be moral and others immoral. It is important to consider the role of Christian theology and the Church in these processes.

II. Same-sex desire in the eyes of theology and the Church

Bishop Burkhard of Worms (d. 1025) evidently had a very physical idea of the 'sin of Sodom'. In his *Decretum*, a penitential intended as an introductory manual for confessors, he offered the following as one of the questions for examination of conscience: 'Have you committed fornication in the manner of the Sodomites by sticking your private member in the rear or back part of a man, thus enjoying coitus like a man of Sodom?'.[12] Here we are offered a realistic image of anal intercourse between two men that should not deflect us into identifying it with the modern idea of 'homosexuality'. On the one hand, the notion of a 'fundamental disposition possibly rooted in human beings'[13] was never associated with it; and, on the other hand, it never occurred to Burkhard to describe mutual masturbation between two men as 'sodomitic'. Other authors attributed quite different associations to this adjective in connection with 'unnatural' forms of sexual intercourse. Even sexual acts between men and women that are not intended to bring about impregnation have sometimes been termed 'sodomitic'. In general, it may be said that in its first ten centuries Christian theology produced no universally applicable and precisely delimited term for same-sex activities.

In any case, the history of interpretation of the story of the destruction of the city of Sodom (Gen 19.1–29) did not concentrate from the start on its sexual aspects. Within scripture the references to Sodom were more directed to the arrogance of its citizens (e.g., Isa. 3.9; Jer. 23.14) or to their refusal to support the poor (Ezek. 16.49f). Even where there are explicit sexual connotations, we are not definitely concerned with same-sex activities (2 Pet. 1.10; Jud. 7f). A gradual contraction to an exclusively 'sexual reading' of the narrative began – among authors recognized by the Church – only with Ambrose and Augustine[14] and finally assumed its fully characteristic form with Gregory the Great (d. 604), when Sodom became the inclusive concept of divine punishment for 'sins of the flesh' (*scelera carnis* – which, truth to tell, are never committed in this particular narrative).[15]

A significant turning-point in this history is reached when Peter Damian (d. 1072), the spokesman for the 'Gregorian reform', coined a new noun in this respect: *sodomia*.[16] This is found in his *Liber Gomorrhianus*, an extensive letter of 1049 to Pope Leo IX. Damian's intention was to arouse the vigilance of Pope and Church on account of the ever-increasing spread of the 'sodomitic curse' among the clergy and religious communities. He was in favour of punishing a 'sodomite' much more strictly than the various penitential manuals had provided for hitherto. His proposals extended from the defrocking of sodomite priests to a death-sentence. These suggestions of Damian's did not meet with immediate success in his lifetime. It was only at the Third Lateran Council in 1179 that some of his recommendations were taken up. Nevertheless, over the years the term 'sodomy' did prevail as a kind of inclusive concept for various sexual actions between men.

Damian developed the word *sodomia* in conscious analogy to *blasphemia*: 'If blasphemy is the worst of sins, I do not know how sodomy could possibly be any better'.[17] Accordingly, from the start 'sodomy' was not a neutral, descriptive term but the theological qualification for a grave sin. Beyond that, the abstract inclusive concept for a series of different behaviours evoked the impression of an essence distilled from these activities: their common characteristic nature. This was to have immense consequences. Henceforth S/sodomites were neither the inhabitants of a town on the Dead Sea nor people who did something which had been imputed to the citizens of Sodom. From now on they were much rather the bearers of the attribute of 'sodomy'. 'They are no longer persons who perform a few similar acts from a myriad of motives, and in incalculably different circumstances. They are Sodomites doing Sodomy.'[18] Thus, a few more or less clearly defined actions gave rise to a specific *type* of human being. Here we have the beginnings of a dichotomy that makes a distinction between sodomites on the one hand and 'normal' people on the other hand, and therefore the beginnings of a way of thinking which, in its wider implications, might well be termed racist.

When the *Summa de poenitentia*, Paul of Hungary's penitential manual, appeared a few decades later, not long after the fourth Lateran Council of 1215, the author had thoroughly adopted the expression 'sodomy' in the meantime. His aim was to convince confessors that it stood for something that was certainly a mortal sin. Evidently there was no consensus of Catholic opinion in this regard: '. . . some count the sin as nothing and . . . in some regions men are abused almost publicly as if from a sort of urbanity (literally, 'courtliness', *curialitas*)'[19] – that, at any rate, was how Paul of Hungary saw things. In his survey of the most important vices, which he classifies in the traditional manner on the basis of the Seven Deadly Sins, he offers an excessively amplified commentary on the 'sin against nature' (allocated to the mortal sin of *luxuria*, 'lust' or 'lasciviousness'). These specific explanations take up about 40 percent of the space for the discussion of all sins whatsoever. Paul uses the term 'sodomy' here as a synonym for 'sins against nature', that is, for a wide range of sexual activities that do not aim at procreation. Any such forms of behaviour are, in his eyes, the reason for famine, plague, and earthquakes. For anything adjudged to be abominable in this regard he provides not only references to the familiar passages in the Bible (Gen. 19; Lev. 18, 20; Rom. 1.26ff), but theological comments: 'Sodomites are the adversaries of God, and murderers and destroyers of humankind. They seem to say to God, "You created human beings to multiply. But we work so that your work may be destroyed"'[20]

Albert the Great (d. 1280) took up this line of argument when he interpreted *luxuria* as *the* sin against the duty of procreation. In his view, the entire amount of available human sperm was precisely equivalent to that required for the survival of the human race. Therefore not one drop of it should be wasted. Albert was probably aware that equating the two in this way did not accord with the medical knowledge of his time, yet he maintained that every seed that did not – in accordance with his teleology – reach a fertile womb represented a mortal sin.[21] Only when he found it necessary to praise the high status of the celibate life was Albert able to disregard his own assertions.

His pupil Thomas Aquinas (d. 1274) did not share these anxieties. In his *Summa theologiae* the Seven Deadly Sins are marginalized and no longer invoked as a systematic framework. Same-sex activities – now those of both men and women – are treated summarily in a subsidiary point of a subsidiary reference.[22] Nevertheless, there is a discrepancy in Thomas's attitude. On the one hand, he removes the topic to a point far from the centre of attention;

on the other hand, he includes 'sins against nature' among the worst of all. On the one hand, he insists on the right use of the powers of procreation for the survival of the species, and then, in his view, true pleasure (*delectatio*) is also available; on the other hand, he acknowledges that even the use of the sexual organs in a way 'contrary to nature' is associated with *delectatio*, which he sees as at least hazardous for the due good order of the soul.

This facing both ways betrays something of the general dilemma that affected medieval theology with regard to these questions: Unlike cases of murder, robbery, or fraud, what exactly is supposed to be so scandalous about same-sex pleasures is not directly evident in any way. On the contrary: for the participants, the *delectatio* provided by same-sex desire is far from slight, and does no injury to other people. Therefore it is not at all revolting, but rather tempting and, not merely for a minority, represents *dangerous desires*. Consequently several penitential manuals advise confessors not to question penitents directly about the sin of sodomy in the confessional, lest they put misleading ideas into their heads. Moreover the theological arguments employed are astonishingly weak and contradictory. In addition to biblical references and invocations of notions of ritual purity, the considerations advanced are constantly centred on the duty of procreation and a teleological determination of the sexual organs as organs of generation.

Other ideas in the texts are possibly more revelatory in terms of background. We often meet with highly prejudiced expressions indicating pollution (*pollutio, turpitudo, obscenus, sordes* etc.), ignominy (*peccatum ignominiosus, flagitium, incontinentia*, indicating the Stoic influence on Paul: *eis pâthé atimías*, Rom. 1.26), and not least of all unmanly behaviour (*mollities, molles,* etc.): 'It is hard to find a single condemnation in the theological tradition that does not rely on misogynistic logic. They condemn violently anything feminine, but especially anything that seems to surrender masculine privilege'.[23]

Here it is important to resist the temptation to seek ready explanations in psychology or cultural criticism. The individual authors, their motives, and their times are too various. Nevertheless, what we can retain from the Middle Ages are not the theological remarks about same-sex desire, but the idea that identity could depend on the sexual organs of the particular sexual partners. The notion that the practice of 'sodomy' makes a person a 'S/sodomite', another kind of human being, is actually a product of Christian theology. Without it the late nineteenth century would never have reached such immediate acceptance of the similar but more extensive concept of 'homosexuality'.

Here 'homosexuality' is not merely the modern translation of the mediaeval term 'sodomy'. When Karol Maria Benkert, an Austro-Hungarian wine-merchant and writer, coined this Greco-Latin neologism in 1869, he associated it entirely with hopes of emancipation. Benkert hoped that inclusion of the term in medical and scientific thought, where it had been traditional since the eighteenth century to assign a biological basis to the otherness of women, blacks or Jews, would lead to a de-moralization of the concept of sodomy. In order to get rid of moral-theological condemnation, it was replaced by the concept of psycho-physical alterity. As a so-to-speak naturally-given *innate disposition*, homosexuality could not be a sin. But this meant that the ultimately problematical theological 'achievement' – the essential alterity of sodomites – actually survived in the form of the biological otherness of 'homosexuals'.

In the Catholic world there was an immediate reaction to the discovery of homosexuality. The notion of an innate disposition was adopted insofar as it helped to demarcate dangerous desire as something of a different type from one's own 'normality'. But at the same time the idea was strongly opposed, insofar as it accompanied the notion of homosexuality as free from any guilt. Within a few decades theological reference works replaced their entries on 'sodomy' with articles on 'homosexuality'. From then on, these articles became constantly more detailed, since now the Catholic position had to be defended against the rival viewpoints of the natural sciences and, soon, of psychoanalysis. This was not achieved without contradictions. For instance, the second edition (1933) of the prestigious Catholic *Lexikon für Theologie und Kirche* declared that, 'It is quite erroneous to derive all cases of homosexuality from a natural disposition and thus to excuse it as one would an illness. . . . That is contrary to the universal moral principle that one is freed from personal responsibility by an innate disposition and passionate inclination only if it occurs as a wholly irresistible compulsion, for otherwise responsibility and sin are at most reduced, but not effaced.'[24]

This introduced a new aspect of the subject into Catholic discourse about homosexuality. What was to be said about 'pre-personal' aspects such as innate disposition, inclination, or instinctive drive? I shall refer here only to one of the increasingly numerous ecclesiastical opinions of recent years: *Homosexualitatis problema*, issued by the Congregation for the Doctrine of the Faith.[24] This document tries to retain the association of innate disposition and behaviour, in order to maintain the condemnation: 'Although the specific inclination of the homosexual person is not sinful in itself it underlies a more or less strong tendency directed to a form of behaviour which is morally wrong. Accordingly, the inclination itself must be treated as disordered' (No.3).

It cannot be said that the argumentation here is any more stringent than in earlier times. Admittedly, there is no longer any mention of earthquake or of spilling of seed, but the notion of the teleology of the sexual organs appears now as the 'complementarity of the sexes', which must reflect the 'inner unity of the Creator'.[25] Nevertheless, the Bible has to do most of the support work for a quite decisive rejection of homosexuality. The objections of exegetes showing that 'no firm scriptural testimony' (No. 5) in this regard is to be found within the Bible are rejected as 'profoundly erroneous and inapt' (No. 4), since Holy Scripture is understood correctly only when it does not contradict the 'living tradition of the Church' (No. 5). Therefore the guiding line for interpretation of the Bible is the tradition whose misinterpretations and strictures in the course of church history first established a reading of the biblical narratives opposed to same-sex desire.

Accordingly, the document demands a multiple intellectual sacrifice (*sacrificium intellectus*): indifference to the findings of biblical science, acceptance of the fiction of a constant scriptural-ecclesiastical position against same-sex desire, and, finally, acquiescence in an understanding of reality in accordance with which 'the practice of homosexuality is a serious threat to the life and well-being of a great number of people' (No. 9).

Even later ecclesiastical standpoints do not move beyond this level of argument. You get the impression of people grasping at every possible straw in order to maintain a position, whereas it becomes increasingly evident that there are no genuine ethical arguments against respectful and non-violent human relationships. The discussion ends here.

III. Summary

Nowadays many liberally-minded people think that they ought to 'accept' the existence of homosexuals; that is, that the valuation of homosexuality has to change. The study of history shows, however, that violence exercised against human desire does not begin with valuation but as early as the stage in which categories are established. The notional division of multiform sexual desire into permissible and prohibited forms of behaviour gives rise to different 'kinds' of people, among whom sodomites *per se* must count as sinful. This is injurious not only to those who are discriminated against by that division, but to all others. For even if the unconscious aim of categorization was probably to ascribe disconcerting sexual feelings to a precisely defined group of 'others', in order to conceive of oneself as 'normal', that does not mean that those feelings are banished in any way. Every human being experiences forms of desire for other people – wholly irrespective of their gender. The occasional appearance of same-sex desires means insecurity and anxiety for many of those who have constructed an unequivocally heterosexual identity in which to enclose themselves. Am I possibly not truly heterosexual? Could I possibly be one of the others, those deviants? If that is so, what will happen to my marriage, or to my position in society?

In many cases such fears give rise to panic defensive reactions (especially among men). By uttering discriminatory statements, and often enough using physical violence against gays and lesbians, individuals who have been made to feel insecure about their sexual identity seek to show themselves and the world that they are 100 per cent on the 'good' side of the dichotomy. They cannot see that it is this very dichotomy that is at the root of their suffering.[26] Those active in homosexual emancipation movements have tried to make positive use within the homo-hetero dichotomy of the role they have been allocated, and to transform it into identity and pride. This strategy has been very successful in many countries. Prohibitions have been removed, anti-discrimination laws have been passed, and forms of legal protection for partnerships have been developed. In this way, the term 'homosexual' has been successfully replaced in certain countries by formerly discriminatory but now politically effective expressions such as 'gay' or 'lesbian'. The price that has had to be paid for all this is the secure inscription of the fundamental alterity of homosexuals in numerous statutory texts, so that many people now think of it as 'natural'. This legally engrossed otherness preserves a demarcation line that can be returned to a state of rigorous severity at any time, should the social climate change.

Therefore I believe that the liberal acknowledgement of the alterity of gays and lesbians does not take us sufficiently far beyond the position of Peter Damian. What we need instead is insight into the artificiality of the terms used to classify human desire, which do equal injury to the existence of 'homosexuals' and of 'heterosexuals'. There are different 'dispositions' just as little as there are different human 'races'. But there are different people. Humans are equal in being different. I agree with Isolde Karle:

'Accordingly, a theology of liberation that can be justifiably invoked here is concerned with nothing less than the liberation of culturally enforced forms of stigmatization experienced by emancipated women, homosexuals, inter-sexuals, and all those men and in-betweens who do not fit into, and suffer from, the current pattern of inherited bourgeois-bipolar sexual typology.'[27]

Perhaps, on this way of liberation from categories and stigmatizations of human origin, it is also possible that we shall recognize God's creation as a gift which includes all human longing – not as something dangerous, but as a power that can produce closeness, solidarity, and love.

Translated by J. G. Cumming

Notes

1. On the first three examples see David M. Halperin, 'Heroes and Their Pals', in: idem, *One Hundred Years of Homosexuality and Other Essays on Greek Love*, New York, 1990, pp. 75–87.
2. Cf. Robert Aldrich, *Gay Life and Culture: A World History*, London, 2006.
3. Tsuneo Watanabe, *The Love of the Samurai*, London, 1989, p. 114, as quoted by Rüdiger Lautmann, '*Homosexualität? Die Liebe zum eigenen Geschlecht in der modernen Konstruktion*', in: Helmut Puff (ed.), *Lust, Angst und Provokation. Homosexualität in der Gesellschaft*, pp.15–37, here 19.
4. Cf. Rüdiger Lautmann, '*Homosexualität?*', *op. cit.*, p. 19. See also: Gilbert Herdt & Robert J. Stoller, *Intimate Communications: Erotics and the Study of Culture*, New York, 1990.
5. Alfred C. Kinsey *et al.*, *Sexual Behavior in the Human Male*, Philadelphia, 1948; id. & Paul H. Gebhard, *Sexual Behavior in the Human Fem*ale, Philadelphia, 1953. One criticism directed against the reports was that the range of subjects questioned about their sexual behaviour was not representative. Accordingly Paul Gebhard, Kinsey's successor as director of the Kinsey Institute for Sex Research, commissioned a project lasting some years to verify the data in the reports and remove any factors that distorted the results. The outcome of these studies, which essentially confirmed Kinsey's conclusions, is available as *The Kinsey Data: Marginal Tabulations of the 1938–1963 Interviews Conducted by the Institute for Sex Research*, Bloomington, Indiana, 1979.
6. Kinsey *et al.*, *Sexual Behavior in the Human Male*, p. 639.
7. *Ibid.*, p. 617.
8. Sigmund Freud, *Drei Abhandlungen zur Sexualtheorie. Die sexuellen Abirrungen*, Leipzig & Vienna, ³1915, p. 5, n. 1 (an additional footnote in the extended edition of 1915). Cf. also, Eng. trans.: *Three Essays on the Theory of Sexuality*, New York, 1962.

9. It was not until 1974 that the American Psychiatric Association removed 'homosexuality' from their official list of psychiatric disorders (*Diagnostic and Statistical Manual of Mental Disorders*). The World Health Organization (WHO) deleted 'homosexuality' from its *International Classification of Diseases* (ICD) only in 1992. On the appreciation and criticism of Freud see Guy Hocquenghem, *Le Désir homosexual*, Paris, 1972, esp. ch. 2.
10. Cf. Isolde Karle, '*Da ist nicht mehr Mann noch Frau...*'. *Theologie jenseits der Geschlechterdifferenz*, Gütersloh, 2006, p. 15.
11. Hocquenghem, *Le Désir homosexuel, op. cit.*
12. *Burchardi Wormaciensis ecclesiae episcopi Decretorum* (Decrees), Libri XX, Decretum XIX, in: J.-P. Migne, *Patrologia Latina*, vol. CXL, 537–1058, in this instance 967D: 'Fecisti fornicationem sicut Sodomitae fecerunt, ita ut in masculi terga et in posteriora virgam tuam immitteres, et sic secum coires more Sodomitico?'
13. Hubertus Lutterbach, *Sexualität im Mittelalter. Eine Kulturstudie anhand von Bussbüchern des 6. bis 12. Jahrhunderts*, Cologne &c, 1999, p. 147. See also the whole chapter on 'Gleichgeschlechtliches sexuelles Verhalten', pp. 147–61.
14. Cf., e.g., Ambrose, *De Abraham*, 1.3.14 and 2.8.45; Augustine, *De civitate Dei* (*The City of God*), 16.30; *Confessiones* (*Confessions*), VIII.15 (In Augustine it is not so much same-sex desire as uncontrolled lust that is to the fore).
15. Cf. Gregory the Great, *Moralia in Job* (*Moral Exegesis of the Book of Job*), 30.18.60; *Regula pastoralis* (*Pastoral Rule*), 3.27. This erroneous interpretation – even more narrowly applied to same-sex acts – has continued until the present day. See, e.g., the 1993 *Catechism of the Catholic Church*, which asserts that 'homosexuality' is called a 'wicked deviation' in Gen. 19 (No. 2357).
16. In this respect I agree with Mark D. Jordan's thesis in his major study *The Invention of Sodomy in Christian Theology* (Chicago & London, 1997).
17. Peter Damian, *Liber Gomorrhianus* (= Epistola 31), in Kurt Reindl (ed.), *Die Briefe des Petrus Damiani* (Monumenta Germaniae Historica 4), vol. 1, Munich, 1983, p. 328.
18. Mark D. Jordan, *Invention of Sodomy, op. cit.*, p. 44.
19. Paul of Hungary, *Summa de poenitentia*, in Bibliotheca Casinensis seu codicum manuscriptorum qui in tabulario casinensi asservantur series . . ., vol. IV (Monte Cassino, 1880), p. 207a.
20. *Ibid.*, 209a.
21. Cf. Albert the Great (Albertus Magnus), *Quaestio de luxuria*, 1–4, in *id.*, *Opera omnia*, ed., Institutum Alberti Magni Coloniense, vol. 25/2, Münster, 1993.
22. Thomas Aquinas, *Summa theologiae*, 2–2. q. 153f. See also: *id.*, *De malo*, 15.1 ad 7 and *Summa contra Gentiles*, 3.122. See Mark D. Jordan, *Invention of Sodomy, op. cit.*, pp. 136ff, for a comprehensive analysis. See Erik Borgman's article in this issue on the understanding of natural law in the Aristotelian-Thomist tradition.

23. Mark D. Jordan, *Invention of Sodomy*, op. cit., p. 169
24. Karl Hilgenreiner, 'Homosexualität,' in: LThK², Freiburg im Breisgau, 1933, pp. 130–1, here 130.
25. Letter of the Congregation for the Doctrine of the Faith to the Bishops of the Catholic Church on the pastoral care of homosexual persons, 30. Oct. 1986.
26. In his article in this issue, Erik Borgman describes how significant changes in emphasis in this respect have taken place from the medieval to the modern eras.
27. Isolde Karle, *'Da ist nicht mehr Mann noch Frau . . .'*, op. cit., p. 12.

Sexual Identity, Culture, Politics: Evaluations

(A) The Moral Values of Europe: Marks or Wounds of Civilization?

JULIE CLAGUE

The European Reform Treaty, agreed by the leaders of the EU Member States in October 2007 and due to come into force in 2009, expresses the vision and values of the European Union as follows:

> The Union is founded on the values of respect for human dignity, freedom, democracy, equality, the rule of law and respect for human rights, including the rights of persons belonging to minorities. These values are common to the Member States in a society in which pluralism, non-discrimination, tolerance, justice, solidarity and equality between women and men prevail.[1]

Thus, the Treaty sets out the moral trajectory and political mission statement of a European Union that comprises 450 million citizens and establishes the next phase of the collaborative effort that is the European Project. Not since the *Universal Declaration on Human Rights* (1948) has there been such an ambitious political effort to characterize and realize the marks of a moral civilization. The Treaty's lofty ideals capture the aspirational goal to do away, once and for all, with the conflicts, grievances, prejudices, nationalisms, and racisms that have afflicted the continent, through the building of a united Europe and the creation of a hospitable and socially inclusive political space that accommodates any lifestyle that can coexist alongside others peaceably.

A vision of a just and good political order based on the same fundamental values is also to be found in the various social teachings of the Roman Catholic Church, and European Catholics – present in each of the twenty-seven Member States – may be reassured to see the strong correspondence between their Church's vision and that laid out in the Treaty. Indeed, in his Apostolic Exhortation, *Ecclesia in Europa*, Pope John Paul II reminded Catholics that they are called to make an 'indispensable contribution to the building in Europe of a civilization ever more worthy of man',[2] and he indicated the applicability of the Church's social teaching in this regard:

> In building a city worthy of man, *a guiding role should be played by the Church's social teaching*. Through this teaching the Church challenges the continent of Europe about the moral quality of its civilization. . . . By the body of principles which it sets forth, the Church's social doctrine helps lay solid foundations for a humane coexistence in justice, peace, freedom and solidarity. Because it is aimed at defending and promoting the dignity of the human person, which is the basis not only of economic and political life, but also of social justice and peace, this doctrine proves capable of upholding the supporting structures of Europe's future.[3]

The prolific papacy of John Paul alone has left a rich legacy of teachings that decry the many social and political injustices that characterize the contemporary world and identify the non-negotiable features that should characterize humankind's common life. Among many other public interventions, he criticized the intolerance that threatens peace by suppressing legitimate social and political pluralism[4] and spoke of the need for legal protections for minorities to prevent discrimination and exclusion.[5] In many respects, therefore, it is possible to see in the statements of these major representatives of humanity, the EU and the Roman Catholic Church, overlapping values and shared concerns. Yet, despite the apparent compatibility of the moral language, John Paul and his successor Benedict have both repeatedly expressed grave misgivings about the aims of the European Project and the values that shape it.

I. The Church's problem with Europe

According to the logic of these two papacies, it is no coincidence that the moral malaise affecting the modern world is writ large in the continent that gave birth to that most influential yet ambivalent of cultural revolutions, the Enlightenment. In its emphasis on the value of freedom, Enlightenment culture has distorted European social life and created an opposition between

The Moral Values of Europe

itself and Christianity.⁶ As a consequence, argues John Paul: '[European] culture is marked by a widespread and growing religious agnosticism, connected to a more profound moral and legal relativism rooted in confusion regarding the truth about man as the basis of the inalienable rights of all human beings.'⁷

A solution is to be found in the Church's social teaching, which, 'contains points of reference which make it possible to defend the moral structure of freedom, so as to protect European culture and society both from the totalitarian utopia of "justice without freedom" and from the utopia of "freedom without truth" which goes hand in hand with a false concept of "tolerance".'⁸

Since the fall of the Iron Curtain in 1989, it is the latter of these two traps that has most taxed the Church. In Pope Benedict's words, there has been a 'degeneration of tolerance into an indifference with no reference to permanent values'.⁹ Paradoxically, he argues, such licence leads not to unlimited freedom for all, but to constraint. Thus, laws prohibiting discrimination can threaten the freedoms of others: 'The concept of discrimination is ever more extended, and so the prohibition of discrimination can be increasingly transformed into a limitation of the freedom of opinion and religious liberty. Very soon it will not be possible to state that homosexuality, as the Catholic Church teaches, is an objective disorder in the structuring of human existence.'¹⁰

In this view, Europe's moral vision is flawed. The values with which the EU intends to fashion a new Europe are not the positive marks of civilization but rather are a symptom of the more fundamental wounds that afflict it. Not surprisingly, therefore, certain legislative proposals put forward by the EU that are seen to promote 'freedom without truth' have met with strong Catholic opposition. The Church's most vehement response has been to legislative efforts within Europe to extend the civil rights of lesbian and gay people.

II. Europe's making or undoing? Legal rights for lesbian and gay people

Across Europe there is greater openness about and acceptance of sexual diversity than at any other time, and this is reflected in unprecedented levels of legal protection for gay and lesbian people. Consenting same-sex intercourse between adults has been decriminalized. Workplace-based sexual orientation discrimination is illegal within the EU. Many – though by no means all – European countries now permit lesbian and gay people to serve openly in the armed forces. A score of nations legally recognize gay partnerships, and the issue is under consideration in Italy, Greece, and Ireland. The Netherlands, Belgium, and Spain have legalized same-sex marriage. Nine of the European countries that extend marriage or partnership rights to same-sex couples allow such couples legally to adopt children.

Nonetheless, the picture remains mixed. Attitudes to homosexualities vary across the European nations. Eastern Europe in particular is less tolerant of alternative lifestyles. In all European nations, prejudice, discrimination, and hate crimes against gay people continue to occur. Europe is far from a safe space to be gay, but there are growing regions of security, toleration, and respectful coexistence. The various EU institutions have been instrumental in transforming the legal frameworks of the Member States. The unacceptability of discrimination on the grounds of sexual orientation was first given explicit mention in article 13 of the EU's *Treaty of Amsterdam* (1997). Since then there has been a gradual though by no means identical legal implementation of this vision across Europe.

Legislation recently enacted in the United Kingdom provides a useful example of the extension of legal rights to gay people. Since 2000 gay people may openly serve in the military. In 2001 the age of consent was equalized. The *Adoption and Children Act 2002* allows same-sex couples jointly to adopt children. *In 2003 the Employment Equality (Sexual Orientation) Regulations* extended protections in the workplace. The *Civil Partnership Act 2004* confers on same-sex couples that register their union the same rights and responsibilities as marriage (some 20,000 couples have registered their unions since December 2005). The *Equality Act 2006* ensures equal treatment in the provision of goods, facilities, and services.

This proliferation of legal protections for gay people in Europe stands in sharp contrast to legal provision worldwide. Same-sex acts remain illegal in seventy-two countries, and may be punishable by death in ten of these. Seen through this wider lens of global attitudes to gay rights it is uncontroversial to state that, as a continent, Europe is furthest advanced in seeking to establish a political community where gay citizens can participate in, contribute to, and benefit from the goods of civil life on a par with their neighbours. For some this represents a substantial moral achievement in a continent where, just decades earlier, gay identity was sufficient grounds for human extermination, alongside other identifiers such as ethnicity and religion. For others, including the official Roman Catholic Church, it signals any number of concerns, including the further erosion of Europe's moral character, a damaging attack on appropriate patterns of human existence as reflected in the basic institutions of social life, a confirmation of the waning of Europe's Christian identity and a rejection of God's will for humanity.

III. The Church's problem with homosexuality

Roman Catholicism proclaims the equal dignity in the eyes of God of all women and men, including lesbian and gay people; homosexuals 'must be accepted with respect, compassion and sensitivity. Every sign of unjust discrimination in their regard should be avoided'.[11] Yet when the Church moves from this general statement to the particulars of how Church and society should guarantee the dignity of homosexual persons, the emphasis shifts dramatically from concerns about how gay and lesbian people might wrongly be subject to negative discriminatory treatment toward assertions of how certain legal restrictions on access to social goods are both morally justifiable and politically necessary. 'Sexual orientation', according to Vatican teaching, 'does not constitute a quality comparable to race, ethnic background, etc. in respect to non-discrimination. Unlike these, homosexual orientation is an objective disorder and evokes moral concern'.[12] Legislation that makes discrimination on the grounds of sexual orientation illegal could have 'a negative impact on the family and society' and should be rejected.[13] According to the Vatican's Doctrinal Note on Catholic participation in political life, such laws 'ignore the principles of natural ethics' and promote freedom of choice 'as if every possible outlook on life were of equal value'.[14] For these reasons, the Church defends the right to discriminate on grounds of sexual orientation.[15]

With regard to civil partnerships, 'the *family* needs to be safeguarded and promoted, based on monogamous marriage between a man and a woman ... in no way can other forms of co-habitation be placed on the same level as marriage, nor can they receive legal recognition as such'.[16] John Paul dismissed attempts 'to accept a definition of the couple in which difference of sex is not considered essential', as one of the many modern threats to marriage and family life that 'jeopardize the truth and dignity of the human person'.[17] In 2003, in a document devoted to the subject, the CDF reiterated that 'the principles of respect and non-discrimination cannot be invoked to support legal recognition of homosexual unions'.[18] On the contrary, 'clear and emphatic opposition is a duty. One must refrain from any kind of formal cooperation in the enactment or application of such gravely unjust laws and, as far as possible, from material cooperation on the level of their application'.[19]

In so saying, the Vatican has placed Catholic hierarchies across Europe on a collision course with their national governments. Bishops must judge how far the Church can become associated with State laws and legalized behaviour of which the Church disapproves without undermining its Christian witness and causing scandal, while taking into account what the political ramifications of non-cooperation might be. As legal provisions for gay people begin to impinge on the practices of Catholics, hierarchies are identifying their national Churches as discriminated parties and appealing to conscience in order to assert the right to religious belief and to defend differential treatment. Across the EU, legal provisions for gay people are creating newly antagonistic Church-State relations. Catholicism finds itself increasingly marginalized: one among any number of potentially competing voices with no power of veto, and offering a vision of life that appears increasingly unappealing to Europe's citizens.

IV. Religious privilege or legal parity? The case of UK Catholic adoption agencies

In the UK, Catholic reaction to the *Equality Act* (which outlaws discrimination on various grounds including sexual orientation) provoked heated debate that divided public and political opinion. The Catholic hierarchies sought to secure special privileges for their adoption and fostering services, which would allow them to refer same-sex couples to alternative agencies. The Cardinal Archbishop of Westminster, Cormac Murphy-O'Connor, head of the Catholic Church in England and Wales, argued that 'to oblige our agencies in law to consider adoption applications from homosexual couples as potential adoptive parents would require them to . . . act against the teaching of the Church and their own consciences', which would be 'unreasonable, unnecessary and unjust discrimination against Catholics'.[20] The Government faced a choice between competing group rights. It could have inserted a clause into the anti-discrimination legislation out of respect for religious belief, which would have exempted Catholic agencies. Instead, the Government opted for consistency within the Act, which offers legal protection from sexual orientation discrimination that is on a par with the protections provided on the grounds of race, gender, disability, and religion. Whereas a number of protections are built into the *Equality Act* to make allowances for differential (e.g., educational) practices on religious grounds, the Government rejected the view that appeal can be made to religious belief where the religious body is in receipt of public funding to provide a social welfare service. Unless the agencies find some means of operating within the law, they will close.

V. The marks of a moral civilization? God and the natural moral law

The Church and the EU both share a desire to build in Europe a truly moral civilization. But the construction of a just political order based on the equal dignity of each, in which everyone can participate and flourish to the fullness of their potential, is no easy task, and it depends for its success on a correct understanding of the human person. Neither political societies nor religious bodies fully respect human dignity and promote human flourishing when the understanding of the person on which they are based is incomplete or flawed. It is for this reason that the Church's problem with Europe and its problem with homosexuality are so closely related. For the Church, 'the truth about man' derives from two mutually reinforcing sources: a correct understanding of God and a correct understanding of the natural moral law; these are the real marks of a moral civilization and both, in the Church's view, have been neglected by Europe: 'When fundamental essentials are at stake: human dignity, human life, the institution of the family and the equity of the social order – in other words the fundamental rights of man – no law made by men and women can subvert the norm written by the Creator in man's heart without society itself being dramatically struck ... at its very core. Thus natural law is a true guarantee for everyone to live freely and with respect for their dignity.'[21]

VI. The Church's natural moral law: Fit for purpose?

For Benedict, natural law is an essential requirement of any moral framework because – in a world where some refute the existence of a shared humanity and reduce morality to mere self- or group interest – it expresses humankind's common moral inheritance and destiny and outlines those features of human living that make the word 'moral' meaningful. It is on natural law grounds that the Church must appeal if it is to convince Europe and the wider world of the truth of its teachings on homosexuality. Natural law arguments are not the only ones that Christians deploy with respect to homosexualities, but it is natural law's supposed universality (unlike the particularity of scriptural and theological claims) that renders it intelligible beyond its own particular religious context and gives it applicability across nations, cultures, creeds, and epochs. So it is claimed. Would that recognizing and interpreting 'the norm written by the Creator in man's heart' were so unproblematic. Natural law's cultural legacy is far from negative. Yet European and ecclesiastical history are replete with examples of wrongful application of natural law reasoning – often by the powerful and privileged, who justified differential treatment that privileged some (often themselves and their associates) and disadvantaged others by claiming that such social arrangements were ordained by God, part of the created order and discoverable by the application of (their own biased) human reason. Whether or not its immutability remains intact, no historical analysis can claim that human reason, over the centuries, has had unhindered access to what the natural moral law demands. This invites caution both on the part of those who claim such knowledge, and on the part of those who proclaim its 'accessibility to all rational creatures'.[22]

The authorized Catholic version of natural law is at its most inaccessible to the power of reasoning and least convincing when applied to sexual morality. To many, a number of its proscriptions appear counter-intuitive; the virtuous person is labelled with vice. This is because what is said to be morally decisive is an action's conformity to reproductive functioning determined by the biological structure of the species. The result is an ontological determinism that fails to capture the richness and complexity of human being and living, diminishes the nature of moral agency, and pre-empts and short-circuits moral reflection. Activity that does not conform to the narrow pattern of acceptable behaviour is considered immoral. Elements such as the person's being of good intention, and the action's circumstances and consequences, which in all other cases give behaviour its moral significance, and which are always relevant for any moral assessment of an action and the person performing it, are in these cases redundant. Thus, same-sex relationships forged in love, faithfulness, and mutuality can be discussed as though they lack any moral qualities, because the realization of these values counts for nothing in the Church's moral evaluation of the behaviour. The Church's natural law-based sexual ethic is a blunt instrument. Moral distinctions are flattened; same-sex love-making and contraceptive love-making are always wrong, irrespective of whether practised as part of a loving committed relationship or an abusive sadomasochistic orgy. In refusing to recognize the existence of goods and values in same-sex relations, and in lumping together and labelling immoral widely differing categories of behaviour (some loving, some abusive, etc.), the Church has highlighted its own crisis of values and lost some of its moral credibility. It is for reasons such as these that many European Catholics find inadequate the Church's teaching on same-sex relationships.

VII. Homosexualities and Catholicisms

Does widespread rejection of such natural law reasoning indicate that Europe has forsaken God? God has not been forgotten by all of secular Europe, though many choose to live as though God did not exist. However, God appears in many different forms for believing Europeans, and not all of these are anti-gay. The official Catholic Church has still to come to terms with the existence of homosexualities. It must also come to terms with the coexistence of Catholicisms within its own ecclesial body, several of which are to be found in Europe.

Loving, committed same-sex relationships and the support, care, companionship, and solidarity that members of the gay community offer to each other amid societal rejection, exclusion, and contempt offer a powerful counter-witness to the culture of selfish individualism and hedonism found within Europe, in which people relate to one another merely instrumentally through self-interested transactions. One hopes that Europe's pioneering support for gay and lesbian people will lead more Christians to recognize that these patterns of living are valuable, and to be celebrated – along with other humanizing expressions of community – as positive features of the human family and an anticipation of God's Holy Polity.

Notes

1. Conference of the Representatives of the Governments of the Member States, *Draft Treaty Amending the Treaty on European Union and the Treaty Establishing the European Community* (CIG 1/1/07 REV 1), Brussels, 5 October 2007, article 2.
2. Pope John Paul II, Post-synodal Apostolic Exhortation, *Ecclesia in Europa*, 2003, n. 105.

3. *Ecclesia in Europa*, n. 98.
4. Pope John Paul II, Message for the XXIV World Day of Peace 'If You Want Peace, Respect the Conscience of Every Person', 1 Jan. 1991, part IV 'Intolerance: A Serious Threat to Peace'. See also part VII 'A Pluralistic Society and World'.
5. Pope John Paul II, Message for the XXII World Day of Peace 'To Build Peace, Respect Minorities', 1 Jan. 1989, n. 4.
6. Cf. Cardinal Josef Ratzinger, Lecture at Saint Scolastica, Subiaco Italy, 1 Apr. 2005. Text available at the website of the Catholic Education Resource Centre under the title 'Cardinal Ratzinger on Europe's Crisis of Culture': http://catholiceducation.org/articles/politics/pg0143.html (accessed 14 October 2007).
7. *Ecclesia in Europe*, n. 9.
8. *Ecclesia in Europa*, n. 98.
9. Pope Benedict XVI, 'Address to Austrian Politicians', Vienna, 8 Sept. 2007.
10. Ratzinger, Lecture at Saint Scolastica.
11. *Catechism of the Catholic Church*, Revised edition 1997, n. 2358.
12. Congregation for the Doctrine of the Faith (CDF), 'Some Considerations Concerning the Response to Legislative Proposals on the Non-discrimination of Homosexual Persons', 1992, n. 10.
13. 'Some Considerations Concerning the Response to Legislative Proposals . . .', Foreword.
14. CDF, 'Doctrinal Note On Some Questions Regarding the Participation of Catholics in Political Life', 2002, n. 2.
15. 'Some Considerations Concerning the Response to Legislative Proposals . . .', n. 11.
16. 'Doctrinal Note On Some Questions Regarding the Participation of Catholics in Political Life', n. 4.
17. *Ecclesia in Europa*, n. 90.
18. CDF, 'Considerations regarding proposals to give legal recognition to unions between homosexual persons', 2003, n. 8.
19. 'Considerations', n. 5.
20. Open letter from Cardinal Murphy-O'Connor to the Prime Minister, Tony Blair, available on the website of the Catholic Church in England and Wales: 'Cardinal writes to the Prime Minister and Members of the Cabinet re. Catholic Adoption Agencies', 22 Jan. 2007; http://www.catholic-ew.org.uk/cn/07/070122.htm (accessed 7 Nov. 2007).
21. Pope Benedict XVI, Address to the International Theological Commission, 5 Oct. 2007.
22. Benedict, Address to the International Theological Commission.

(B) Homosexuality in South Africa

CHARLES RYAN

I. The Past

In Apartheid-era South Africa the law enshrined a deep-seated homophobia. The National Party, the party which pioneered the notion and practice of Apartheid, had inherited a system which made sodomy – defined as oral or anal sex between men – a crime. The notorious 'Immorality Act' of 1957 had further prohibited men from engaging in 'any erotic conduct' when there were more than two people present. The Sodomy Law of 1976 declared homosexuality a crime that was punishable by imprisonment of up to seven years. Specific laws were enacted to 'prevent' homosexuality, for example, in the South African Defence Force, providing for various medical procedures aimed at changing sexual orientation.

II. The Present

Whether or not it was a conscious reaction to the extreme intolerance of the Apartheid era, the ANC-led government that was installed at the beginning of democracy in 1994 moved quickly to remove virtually all restrictive laws, especially in the area of sexual morality. Section 9 of chapter 2 of the new Constitution of South Africa (dated 8 May 1996) states: 'The state may not unfairly discriminate directly or indirectly against anyone on one or more grounds, including race, gender, sex, pregnancy, marital status, ethnic or social origin, colour, sexual orientation, age, disability, religion, conscience, belief, culture, language and birth.' Article 10 of the same Constitution says: 'Everyone has inherent dignity and the right to have their dignity respected and protected.'

Apart from the general outlawing of 'unfair discrimination' on the basis of 'sexual orientation' specific laws were enacted to make the rights of homosexual persons more explicit. As early as 1993 the African National Congress

(ANC) had endorsed legal recognition of same-sex marriages, and it went on to pass a series of relevant liberating laws:

In 1999 unregistered cohabitation of same-sex couples was legalized. That 'permission' was strengthened when the National High Court, sitting in Bloemfontein, ruled in July 2002 that denying same-sex couples the right to marry was discriminatory and thus unconstitutional. When the matter was referred to the Constitutional Court of South Africa, they ruled in December 2005 that preventing same-sex marriages was unconstitutional, and they instructed Parliament to enact laws accordingly. The laws were enacted by a vote in parliament on 1 December 2006, the voting being 230 for, 41 against, and three abstentions. Thus South Africa became the sixth country in the world and the first in Africa to legalize same-sex marriages.

The Child Care Act of 1983 had prevented same-sex couples from adopting children, but when the Act was challenged by du Toit and de Vos, the Constitutional Court, on 18 September 2002, stated that 'people in permanent same-sex partnerships could provide children with a stable home and the support and affection necessary', thus effectively abrogating the 1983 Act.

In 1998 the Employment Equity Act was passed to prevent unfair labour discrimination on the basis of sexual orientation. In 1999 the country recognized same-sex partners' rights to immigration, and in 2002 it granted same-sex partners the same financial benefits as married heterosexual partners.

Finally, the South African Parliament is currently (November 2007) processing a comprehensive law that will remove all criminal content from sexual activity between consenting adults – either heterosexual or homosexual – and the age of adulthood is set at sixteen years. Previously the age of consent had been set at sixteen for heterosexual sex, but at nineteen for homosexual acts.

In other words, from the constitutional and legal perspectives South Africa has one of the most liberating and liberated regimes in the world in the matter of homosexuality.

III. Some Problems

Even if, as one newspaper article says: 'South Africa now has one of the most progressive constitutions in the world as far as gay rights are concerned',[1] it cannot be assumed that the South African society is as tolerant as the constitution and laws would imply. Traditional African societies, all over Africa, are notoriously intolerant of homosexuality. This is probably associated with a very basic instinct to ensure the perpetuation of a particular ethnic group, and homosexuality, being non-generative, does not promote this end. South Africa, because of its long association with foreign cultures and practices, and with its longer history of industry and urbanization than any other African nation, has experienced the phenomenon of open gay relationships since the advent of mining and single-sex worker hostels away from the traditional communities. However, all such phenomena were viewed as 'un-African' and assumed to be practices that were introduced by foreign – non-African – people.[2] With the collapse of Apartheid 'Africanness' is once more honourable, so it is politically correct to condemn un-African values. Thus, the incidence of violence and discrimination against homosexual persons is still extremely high, especially in traditional African communities of South Africa and, even more seriously, in the urbanized black communities where traditional discipline has collapsed but remnants of traditional 'instincts' have survived.

The problem of violence, especially in the economically challenged urban settlements – previously referred to as 'townships'[3] – is a topic of much current debate. However, there is no denying that the incidence of murder, rape, armed robbery, hijacking of cars, child abuse, and so on has reached frightening proportions. One particularly obnoxious belief, resulting in the rape of large numbers of female children, states that to have sex with a virgin is a cure for Aids. Of almost the same cynicism is the belief, also commonly held, that a lesbian woman can be cured of her 'abnormality' by being raped by a man. This results in frequent rapes, perpetrated even by schoolboys, of girls who show signs of rejecting heterosexual liaisons. Because of political implications statistics are not available or reliable, but the reality of widespread discrimination and violence against homosexual persons is undisputed.

Some examples: On Sunday 8 July 2007 a lesbian outreach worker with the Positive Women's Network (PWN) and her friend Salome Masooa were brutally raped and murdered in Soweto. The two had been first tortured and finally shot in the head.[4] The national press reported the murders, but there has been no subsequent report of arrests. An anonymous bystander interviewed by the *Sunday Times* newspaper said: 'there is no place here for such people (the lesbians)'

On Thursday 11 October 2007 the *Natal Witness* reported that a banner had appeared in a local community inviting people to join a cultural organization, with the concluding words (in Zulu): '*Siyabonga Ngezitabane*'. The words literally mean 'thank you, homosexuals', but in the context they mean 'homosexuals, thank you for not joining'. The banners were challenged by the local representative of the Gay and Lesbian Network, who reported the situation to the Pietermaritzburg branch of the South African Human Rights Commission. The response of the person responsible for erecting the banners is reported to have been 'they can go ahead (with the report). I don't care'.

Similar reports of violence and discrimination are not rare. However, even if bureaucracy and lack of motivation hinder the implementation of the anti-discrimination laws, Gay Rights activists do have a forum for airing their grievances and can hope for a gradual improvement through energetic advocacy work. In this respect South Africa is still unique in Africa.

IV. Christianity and Homosexuality in South Africa

When same-sex unions were legalized by Parliament in Cape Town in 2006 one Kenneth Meshoe, referred to as a 'Christian legislator', said that it was the 'saddest day in our twelve years of democracy'. He warned that South Africa was 'provoking God's anger'.[5] Meshoe's reaction might well be described as 'fundamentalist', but the fundamentalist approach can also be found in the folds of the more established denominations!

On 20 March 2006 this writer was a member of a small panel that convened in Durban to discuss an appropriate response from the Catholic Church in South Africa to the imminent legalizing of same-sex unions. The meeting was chaired by a very senior leader of the Church. In a written submission I suggested that the Church should:

(1) Try as hard as possible to prevent the word 'marriage' being used for same-sex unions;
(2) Await the text of the proposed law from Parliament before reacting;
(3) Agree that there is no problem with an agreement that shares assets, inheritance rights, etc. between same-sex partners;
(4) Obtain empirical information about the possible damage to children adopted or otherwise introduced into same-sex partnerships; and
(5) Develop a clear, non-judgmental catechesis on homosexuality for Catholics (since it was clear at the time that the law was going to be passed regardless of any opposition).

When the law was eventually passed in December of the same year, one can only imagine the surprise when the most popular Sunday newspaper in

South Africa, the Johannesburg *Sunday Times*, appeared with banner headlines proclaiming the Catholic Church's opposition to the law and quoting Cardinal Wilfred Napier, the archbishop of Durban, saying that same-sex marriage 'is doomed to have a morally deleterious effect on the institution of the family' and would mean 'the approval of deviant behaviour' and would 'send the wrong message by making acceptable what is repugnant'. The Cardinal's words and a statement from the South African Bishops' Press Office[6] reminded the public that passing a law approving same-sex marriages 'does not make them morally right' for 'no one can go against God's will and come unscathed'. Threatening God's punishment and using words like 'deviant' and 'repugnant' is hardly the way to convey the vision of a compassionate non-judgmental Christian Saviour.

History in South Africa is unfolding in much the same way as it has done in Western Europe and USA. Homosexual persons have organized themselves into advocacy and welfare groups. They have also separated themselves from 'straight' society by occupying certain suburbs in the large cities such as Johannesburg and Cape Town and identifying welcoming meeting places, such as hotels, clubs, and bars in smaller centres, where they can function as an unchallenged sub-culture and feel reasonably secure. They do not feel welcome in mainline Churches but congregate religiously in a small number of independent churches that have expressed a welcome for homosexuals. Some of the fundamentalist denominations conduct sporadic demonstrations with banners and loudspeakers at known homosexual meeting-places, but they are careful not to contravene the law, so a reasonably peaceful co-existence prevails.

The issue of homosexual clergy is being openly discussed in the Anglican Church of South Africa. This is nothing but a reflection of the ongoing debate in the Anglican Communion around the world and the controversies in USA, Canada, and Nigeria. In 2002 a survey was conducted among priests and pastors of seven different denominations in South Africa[7]. The results were predictable in that the Anglican Church leaders showed themselves to be engaging with homosexuality and trying to be inclusive of homosexual persons in the Church. The Catholic priests interviewed were unanimous that homosexuals should be welcome in the Church but on the well-known Catholic condition that they live celibate lives (either as clergy or lay people). The United Reformed Church, Presbyterian Church, and Dutch Reformed Church (the denomination mostly associated with the conservative morality of the Apartheid era) were, in that order, the least welcoming to homosexuals, and this was reflected in the answers that were geared to measuring the extent of pastoral care available to homosexual persons in the various Churches. It seems the ecclesiastical leopards have not changed their spots in South Africa! The most important issue related to the survey is that the matter of homosexuality is being discussed in a reasonably dispassionate way. This must be seen as a good side effect of the open discussion of homosexuality in particular and sexuality in general that has become necessary in a country that is escaping from the repressions and horrors of Apartheid, while engaging with the tragedy of having almost six million HIV-positive citizens, the majority of whom belong to cultures that forbid any open discussion about sexuality.

V. Theology and Homosexuality in South Africa

Given the Catholic Church's centralized statements on issues like homosexuality, and given the history of Catholicism's status as a minority and somewhat feared denomination since that country's colonial era, it is not surprising that theological speculation on homosexuality is virtually confined to re-stating the position found in documents like the *Catholic Catechism* and the 1975 *Declaration on Certain Questions concerning Sexual Ethics* from the Congregation for the Doctrine of the Faith.[8] 'Homosexual acts are intrinsically disordered' and therefore '... under no circumstances can be approved'[9].

In 2006 I was invited to a gathering of priests and religious working in the area of formation of seminarians and others in one of South Africa's provinces. The assignment was to introduce them to the recently-promulgated Instruction from the Congregation for Catholic Education about 'People with Homosexual Tendencies' in seminaries and other institutions. I pointed out that the document had listed: (1) 'those who practice homosexuality', (2) those who 'present deep-seated homosexual tendencies' and (3) those who 'support the so-called gay culture'[10] as unacceptable, but the document equally had not totally excluded homosexual persons. Therefore, I pointed out, we must not be 'more Roman than Rome'. This gave rise to an emotional outburst from one of the participants that 'next, you will be advocating that we have sex with animals!' Apparently, homophobia is alive and well in the Catholic Church in South Africa.

It is in the Anglican Church in South Africa that any significant theological speculation and discussion is taking place. Archbishop Desmond Tutu, the Nobel Peace Prize winner and still-active advocate of reconciliation and dialogue among the various groupings in South Africa, was interviewed on South African TV when the controversy over ordination of homosexual people in USA and Canada was at its climax. When asked about homosexuality in the clergy in the Anglican Church in South Africa he smiled and said: 'It is not an issue with us!' However, while Tutu's view might be an oversimplification, there appears to be no danger of a split as in other countries. The Church does have its so-called 'Trads' and 'Chads'[11], the 'Trads' (traditionalists) wanting to retain the traditional interpretations of scripture and the inherited disciplinary practices about homosexuality, while the 'Chads' want changes both in the interpretation of scripture and toward more openness to homosexual people in the Church.

VI. An Experiment

In Semester II of the 2006 academic year I taught a course on sexuality and marriage in one of South Africa's Catholic Theology Institutes. The students came from eleven African countries and were mostly from traditional (as distinct from urbanized) backgrounds. Apart from dealing with the usual inhibitions in discussing matters of sexuality I also became aware of a certain preoccupation with (if not fear of) the issue of homosexuality. I therefore decided to address the issue in some detail from the psychological, scriptural, and theological perspectives. After the treatment, I invited the students to summarize what they now say about homosexuality, and the result was the following twenty 'theses':

1. Every human person is created in the likeness of God and therefore is equally worthy of respect. This includes homosexual people.
2. Homosexuality is 'there'. It exists in every culture and every ethnic group, even if it is concealed. Denial of its existence in particular cultures is common.
3. The precise cause of homosexuality is not understood. It may be genetic, environmental or a combination of both, or something else. It is very rarely freely chosen.
4. Psychiatry and Psychology do not consider it a pathology that requires treatment.
5. A distinction must be drawn between homosexuality as an orientation and homosexual activity.

6. Surveys suggest that between 6% and 15% of the human population experience homosexual tendencies.
7. There is no reliable external indicator of someone being homosexual, in spite of stereotypical thinking being very common.
8. Celibacy is a challenge as well as a charism. The challenge is the same for a heterosexual as for a homosexual person.
9. Paedophilia is a psychological problem. There is no basis for identifying it more with homosexual persons than with heterosexual persons.
10. The Catholic Church has always condemned sex outside marriage. Overt heterosexual and homosexual (genital) activity are both included in the general condemnation.
11. The Church does not accept same-sex unions because (a) 'they are unnatural' and (b) they are not 'open to procreation'.
12. Homophobia is a reality in most societies. This can result in decisions by homosexual persons that are not appropriate, e.g. entering into a homosexual culture, being heterosexually promiscuous or entering into a heterosexual marriage to 'deflect suspicion'.
13. Self-esteem and self-acceptance are crucial in the life of everyone, but extremely difficult for a homosexual person because of homophobia. Counselling can be of great value in this regard.
14. While there are minority contrary views, it is regarded as not possible to change one's sexual orientation.
15. A well-articulated and balanced modern theology of sexuality is hard to access. However, Pope Benedict's Encyclical *Deus Caritas Est* (2005) is an example of the Church truly searching for such a theology.
16. It must be possible for a homosexual person to own and embrace his/her orientation. The alternative is a life of low self-esteem.
17. As in all other moral matters conscience must be respected and given its appropriate status when relating to persons of homosexual tendencies. Ultimately, only the subject may judge conscience.
18. It must be realized that external standards of behaviour are appropriate in religious and secular communities. Imposing such standards is not judging, but it must be done with sensitivity and respect.
19. It must also be realized that certain secular authorities, such as the government of South Africa, have made any form of discrimination on the basis of sexual orientation illegal. The Church must take account of these laws.
20. Paraphrasing the New Testament incident where Jesus was asked about

the blindness of the man born blind, it should also be possible to say that someone's homosexuality is not caused by the sins of parents or the sin of the subject, but 'so that the works of God might be revealed in him' (John 9.1–3). The works of God will be revealed when a homosexual person is able to live 'the fullness of life' in an unstigmatizing Church and society.[12]

VII. Conclusion

The unique history of South Africa has produced a society that has enshrined unusually 'liberal' laws about homosexuality. However, the reality is that homophobia, denialism, discrimination and prejudice are still at work in the secular life of the country and in the Churches, including the Catholic Church. Intemperate utterances by civil and church leaders will not result in a society that is inclusive of homosexual people. The Jesus whom Christians follow asked us not to judge and to be compassionate as our Heavenly Father is compassionate. Homosexuality might well be the one remaining frontier that must be conquered with Christ's compassion and not by moralizing and judging.

Notes

1. 'Mom, I'm gay', an anonymous article published in the *Natal Witness*, a respected South African daily newspaper, 25 Apr. 2006, p.13.
2. Discussions about the possibility of homosexuality being equally found in traditional communities, even if concealed, are frequently met with angry rejection, even if no empirical evidence is available to support or reject such a notion.
3. The world at large has heard much about the notorious Johannesburg township called 'Soweto' (South West Township), but may not know that every 'white' town in Apartheid South Africa had one or more townships nearby. Those were the communities where the black workers lived and from which they commuted to work for the white employers. Fourteen years after democracy, the phenomenon still persists.
4. http://www.blacklooks.org
5. B. A. Robinson, 'Same-sex marriage: Recognition of Same-Sex Partnerships and Marriages in South Africa', 2006; http://www.religioustolerance.org.
6. C. Townsend (Press Officer for South African Catholic Bishops Conference), *Initial Statement of the Catholic Bishops of S.A. on Same-sex unions*, 2006.
7. IAM (Inclusive and Affirming Ministries), *A survey amongst clergy of 7 denominations in South Africa – on their attitude towards, knowledge of, exposure and*

pastoral approach to Homosexuality, 2002. http://www.cpsajoburg.org.za/socres/sexuality
8. It is also important to note that the number of Catholic theologians, and particularly moral theologians, in South Africa is extremely small.
9. *Catechism of the Catholic Church*, n. 2357.
10. See Congregation for Catholic Education, *Instruction Concerning the Criteria for the Discernment of Vocations with regard to Persons with Homosexual Tendencies in view of their Admission to the Seminary and to Holy Orders*. 4 Nov. 2005, n. 2.
11. I am indebted to Professor Kevin Balkwill, head of the School of Animal, Plant and Environmental Sciences at the University of Witwaterand in Johannesburg (and a post-graduate student of theology), for the ideas in this paragraph. He also supplied the following valuable bibliographical material about the discussion of homosexuality in the Anglican Church in South Africa:

    Bishops of the Province of Southern Africa (Anglican). *Statement from the Anglican Church on Marriage and Same-sex Relationships*. 2005. http://www.cpsajoburg.org.za/bishsynetc
    South African Anglican Theological Commission. *The Church and Human Sexuality*. Cape Town, 1992.
    South African Anglican Theological Commission. *Anglicans and Sexual Orientation*. Cape Town, 1997

12. There was one dissenter among the twenty-six students who produced this. He was uncomfortable with what he termed 'misuse' of scripture in the last thesis. I obtained permission from the students to use this.

(C) 'The Silent War': How Latin American Women can be What They Want

NANCY CARDOSO PEREIRA

I shall be a saint, be a horse, be a bougainvillea! a union boss!
I shall be a winged old lady! a man and a woman: I shall be what I want!
I shall be invisible! I shall be a blind seer! a sleepwalker! an animal!
I shall see in the dark! I shall be a lawyer-father-camel!
I shall be luminous!

Manuel Scorza recounts that a certain man, a powerful magistrate in a province in the Peruvian Andes, let a 1 *sol* coin fall to the ground . . . and for a year no one dared to touch it. The coin stayed there, intact, paralyzed by all the people's fear. This magistrate's wife loved organizing parties – lots of parties! – and, coming to the conclusion that twelve months was far too long to wait to celebrate her next birthday, decided to speed time up: so she shortened the year, cutting down the months so that she could have two or three birthday parties a year. . . . Scorza's conclusion is: 'America's so-called fantastic literature is simply realist. The excesses are not in the literature but in the reality.'[1]

One of the most expressive aspects of Latin-American cultures – 'magic realism' – embraces a series of writers from different Latin latitudes and various times, each with their narrative originality but with some features in common: magic realism produces works about reality without claiming to hold a mirror up to the actual reality. Fantastical writings, the unreal, and the magical imagination are epistemic and narrative fables that discuss ways of approaching the reality of Latin America while negating the commercialization of discourse on identity: '. . . the fantastical text is political, not because it deals with any extraordinary political event, but because it refers to a particular literature and debates with the condition of art as merchandise.'[2]

So, when Manuel Scorza writes about the land-owning structure of Peru, he notes that hedges spring out of the ground – hedges enclosing private property advance on the communal lands like very violent living beings: 'It was weeks since the hedge had come to birth in the meadows of Rancas.' Men ran about, fearful of being caught ' by that worm that had an advantage over human beings: it never ate, never slept, never tired'. Many people prayed 'in the fields, terrified', since there was nowhere left for them to run to. 'The inhabitants of the lowlands could disappear into the forests or climb the mountain ranges. But they lived on the roof of the world.' There was nothing else it could be: 'that hedge is the devil's work'.[3]

With the coming together of economic, theoretical, political, and cultural monoculture, reading Latin American magic realism can be a necessary exercise in re-taking possession of critical matrices invalidated by the inventors of the homogeneity of Latin American identity.

We women of Latin America are many – so many. Ground down by the forces of mercantilist and Christian colonization, the many faces of Latin America were massacred, first for the sake of projects of conquest, then by projects of nationhood, which ignored and rode roughshod over the conditions and ways of life of the native peoples. Throughout the continent, the majorities still carry on with their lives filled with magic reality: their survival as peoples who can tell their stories has been the greatest miracle.

These peoples have their narratives and their historical and cultural forms of self-expression. These make up the conditions and emotions that nourish the historical resistance and struggles for liberation on the continent of Latin America. Caught up in a violent process of class struggle on the periphery of international capital, these narratives and their ways of life oscillate between origins and modernity, old and new, value and non-value as a permanent conflict: 'the open veins of Latin America'.

The conflict is also situated in the processes of political critique and struggle, in the question of what place these founding narratives with their myths of resistance have and can have in the liberation project for the continent, contributing to a socio-economic model that reconciles people and territory without the constraints of enslaving controls that keep us on the periphery of the power structures of the world's ruling classes.

The historic utopias of a 'Great Nation' of Latin America, followed by the independence processes, hardly ever had the patience and wisdom to listen to possible replies to these questions, overlaying projects of nation- or continent-hood that ignored the actual fantastic realities of the majorities. The revolutionary projects that originated in Latin America were nourished directly by the magic realism of the indigenous, Afro-American, and peasant people. The theoretical and programmatic formulations of some movements proved a further source of violence, owing to their inability to construct a dialogue between the structures of the magic realism of other areas of the world and the plurality of struggles and identities of the peoples of Latin America. 'In the case of Latin America, innumerable identities stemming from others have been constructed, starting with the name "Latin America" itself, which is no more than a term coined by Louis Napoleon Bonaparte to designate the territory he proposed to conquer, making it the view of a ruler conceiving an identity totally alien to the people who composed its societies.'[4]

Magic realism is at one and the same time a narrative technique and an experimental instrument for situating its readers on the border between normality and abnormality, with an ability to reveal the mechanisms that configure discourses on reality and its conflicts. Literature uncovers the fables beneath reality, its fissures, its most imperfect joints, generating a vital epistemological doubt: true or false, possible or impossible? 'So it imparts an ambiguity that becomes a third element and whose meaning is, in itself, its very ambiguity. In this way, the commonest interpretation of this ambiguity is provided by understanding it as allegory, and in this sense the deciphering of this allegory comes to reveal, behind the "fictional construct of reality", reality (itself).'[5]

Latin American liberation theology, with its passion for the poor and their revolutionary movements, has also familiarized itself with this fantastical literature, becoming literate in the words the people invent but also taking critical account of the powerful concepts and suggestions contained in this literature. This conversation has not always proved fruitful; certain theological constructs have been unable to bear the longer journey taken by literature, preferring the analytical and descriptive language of critical science. 'Nevertheless, this theology ended up imprisoned by the social sciences and abandoning important aspects of the life of the poor, including their bodies and sexual practices. . . . First-generation liberation theologians were ill-equipped for dealing with bodies brimming over with desires and sexualities in the midst of poverty. The literature of liberation theology seems to show what is not explicit in its texts, that is, that our theologians do not possess the tools for working on these questions, do not have the eyes to discern them, the theological categories in which to rationalize them, or even the challenging imagination to envisage the existence of such matters.'[6]

In the wake of the so-called 'liberation of theology', discourses and actions are no longer imprisoned in ready-made and oft-repeated formulas to express reality, finding one of their most creative methodological challenges in their exchanges with the literature of magic realism. In Bishop Pedro Casaldáliga's words:

> And these poets impress me deeply: they have the passion of the Celt-Iberians, the overflowing imagination of the great mountain ranges, of the mighty rivers, of that nature we lack in Spain. At the same time, most of them possess that half-secret symbolism of mysticism, of the word, and of the silence of the indigenous peoples. Latin American novelists are highly symbolic: they cross the action, the plots of their novels, cross them with symbols, with myths.
>
> I find two great poets among the novelists of Latin America: García Márquez and the volcanic writing of the Peruvian Manuel Scorza. Scorza labours more explicitly at words and passion than García Márquez. Both, however, maintain a very high standard. They show the two parameters of which I spoke. On one side, there are some who restrict themselves somewhat, shall we say, to the realm of socialist realism; on another, a vast array who seek to invent a language suitable to the continent.[8]

This language could be the sickly and repeated sensuality of Gabriel García Márquez's Sierva María de Todos los Ángeles (Servant Mary of All Angels) in *El amor y otros demonios*, with her little mouth eating unending grapes: 'Sierva María was sitting in front of a window that gave on to a snow-covered landscape, pulling off and eating one by one the grapes from a bunch she held in her lap. Each grape she pulled off promptly grew again on the bunch. In the dream, it was clear that the girl had spent many years in front of that infinite window, trying to finish the bunch, but that she was in no hurry, knowing that death was in the last grape.'[9] However, I have chosen Manuel Scorza's *La guerra silenciosa* (The Silent War), as being at once a detailed diary of the indigenous and peasant uprisings that started in Peru in the 1950s and a mosaic of the impossible beliefs that sustained the people in the midst of their historical and personal setbacks. These are dazzling accounts of real failures, with the element of fantasy splitting apart the arrogant reality and discipline of the victors and allowing the inadequate bravery of the vanquished to creep into the narrative. This is no heroic dramatization of the historic failures of indigenous and peasant people in Latin America, but it does deal with the everyday and fantastic production of the glorious miracle of their resistance in bodies seized with hunger and cold but also with love and desire.

The magical language of magical beings in a truly magical natural setting needs real bodies, and it this bodily materiality of the stories, of the possibilities springing from bodies that strip off fixed identities and present Indians and peasants as beings full of ambiguity – with a vulnerability and ambiguity so ancient, so traditional, so customary that they will not allow the poor to be finally massacred either by history or by myths. In that and this 'Silent War' we women of Latin America can be what we want!

I. The Silent War: the books and their characters

During the 1970s Manuel Scorza wrote a narrative cycle, known as 'The Silent War', whose backdrop was the indigenous and peasant movements fighting for land in Peru. Based on historical facts, documentary fragments and news items concerning these events, Scorza produced five novels: *Redoble por Rancas* (Drumroll for Rancas, 1970); *Garabombo, el invisible* (The invisible Garabombo, 1971); *El jinete insomne* (The sleepless horseman, 1977); *Cantar de Agapito Robles* (Song of Agapito Robles, 1977); and *La tumba del relámpago* (The lightning's tomb, 1979). Scorza himself explains: *Redoble por Rancas* is the individual revolt; *Garabombo, el invisible* the collective revolt; *El jinete insomne* the rekindling of courage, a tactical withdrawal in the struggle [. . .]; *Cantar de Agapito Robles* returns to the collective endeavour and reflects a provisory triumph; *La tumba del relámpago* is the book of clarity, the acquisition of a collective consciousness.[10]

Against the backdrop of five hundred years of European occupation, now embodied in the dominance of North American capitalist enterprises, the indigenous communities live away from their own lands, driven like animals into the hills and surviving cold and hunger. Many find work in the mines, perpetuating their alienation from their territory for the sake of the economic interests of Peruvian and foreign elites. Writing about this situation implies, for Scorza, intervening in it, choosing one's materials, opting for narrative instruments that are also interpretative and political. Scorza's political horizon and his re-readings of the Peruvian communist activist Mariátegui are evident: 'The indigenous question springs from our economy. It has its roots in the land-ownership system. Any attempt to resolve it through administrative or police measures, through teaching methods or efforts at empowerment, will turn out to be superficial or adjectival, as long as the feudalism of the local chiefs remains unchanged.'[11]

By choosing magical narrative Scorza is not reproducing – or trying to! – the mythical universe of the indigenous peoples, nor bending to the orthodox thinking of Latin American communism aligned with Moscow's propaganda. There is a specificity of the indigenous world that needs to be known, analyzed, and interpreted on the basis of class struggle as dialectic of the materiality of history. This need for the materiality of the class struggle, its incarnation in a time and space belonging to actual unique and unrepeatable people, places the Indian ancestral modalities in relation to power structures, not as praise of a lost past but as possible grounds for historical construction. In Scorza's words:

> Driven out of time and space, the survivors of pre-Columbian cultures take refuge in the only territory open to them: myth. Because a people driven out of history can return to history not through history, but only through myth. Myth is the armour that will protect their wounded selves, the shell that will defend the soft flesh of their future being, the identity they wait for in the future. Because in certain cases the history of a people lies not in their yesterday but in their tomorrow. In America, myth is not a literary request: it is an imperious historical construction, a necessity for human existence, the skeleton that will support the flesh of the recovered word.[12]

These relationships between myth and history will be lived out by Scorza's characters in a fantastical fashion, without being in any way exhausted in formulas of identification, programming, or theorizing. In the 'Indians in themselves – Indians for themselves' plot, Scorza draws out concepts and language into 'Indians in themselves – class for themselves'. His characters will be built up on fantastical lines, full of unreality in their real fictional bodies. Scorza's people can be what they want to be! They are completely taken into and submerged in the ancestral way of life; they are completely weakened and vulnerable in relation to the power ploys of absentee landlords and capitalists, as well as in relation to the theories and programmes of pre-fabricated revolutions.

Full of ambiguity, social subjects can be what they want, what they need to be as unexpected arrangements of personal will and collective will, of personal need and of collective need. To complete the extension of possibilities, they continue to be inexorable in history and time themselves. Time for! Narrative can do this: 'It is a case of non-chronological narration of events. The narrative progress ceases to be linear and is broken constantly by interruptions and leaps forward or back in time. The course of the chronologically fractured novels carries in itself a conception of a rhythm that smacks of the story-telling technique of the collectivity the cycle of novels deals with, the Quechua peasantry.'[13]

II. The characters' possibilities

The main characters in each novel in 'The Silent War' sequence are the indigenous communities, which are shown in their geographical setting and in their ways of life: food, work, family relationships, community relationships, devotion, sexuality and so on. But it is through his accounts of individuals that Scorza develops his construction of the historical subject of insurrection. In each of the novels, there are one or more personages who take on the characteristic of total incarnation in the indigenous framework, displaying its special, fantastical, conditions or characteristics.

In *Redoble por Rancas*, Héctor Chacón can make things out in the night as well as he can in the day; in *Garabombo el invisible*, Fermín Espinosa suffers from invisibility only to the eyes of the powerful; in *El jinete insomne*, Raimundo Herrera never sleeps; in *El cantar de Agapito Robles*, Agapito can change himself into an animal; in *La tumba del relámpago*, Genaro Ledesma has nothing fantastic about his appearance but is destined to be the one who gives the community back the collective consciousness of the struggle itself.

These special powers are at once expressions of the situation of oppression in which the indigenous people live and life-giving strategies in the process of organizing the struggle. So with Garabombo, the invisible man: his invisibility denounces the total defencelessness and inexistence of the indigenous communities in the eyes of the authorities and the powerful. As the narrative unfolds, Garabombo uses his invisibility in the service of the community; he goes in and out of offices and military quarters in such a way as to be able to acquire information to be used in the struggle. When the communities rise up and the confrontation begins, Garabombo ceases to be invisible . . . as do the people also! 'They were seeing him! The crowd breathed out something woven from relief, rejoicing, and anguish. They were seeing him! Garabombo was fulfilling his promise: he was visible. No one would conquer them! "Neither herbalists nor witches will cure me. The day you are brave, I shall be cured! The day I command the communal cavalry!" A certainty stronger than the rocky fastnesses drove them forward' (p. 195).

Raimundo Herrera, the sleepless knight, caught the curse of sleeplessness in 1705, when the communities' lands were seized. Time stopped for him and he was cured of his infirmity only 275 years later, on the day the community decided to fight to get its land back. This total simultaneity between the collective and the individual is an important part of Scorza's narrative and serves to explicitate the formation of a class consciousness within the indigenous consciousness itself. This process of formation is full of contradictions, of ambiguities, and of failures, which are being overcome in history without any tolerance of idealizations or individualizations of social subjects. In Gerardo Ledesma all the previous appearances are expressed as capacity for judgment, organization, and leadership in the political struggle. While he is the character devoid of fantastical elements, Genaro gathers into himself all the potentialities of the other characters: he sleeps little; he needs to come and go without being seen by the authorities; he moves from advocacy to leadership of and political spokesman for the community; he needs to see by day and by night, keeping his capacity for discernment in the course of the indigenous uprising.

This process takes place in the bodies of the characters. The actual scenario in which the subjects are formed is made up of corporealities, of the materialities shared by all human beings, but which, affected by the liberation struggle, rise above the limitations set by custom or nature. Bodies exceed themselves! Bodies are transfigured in themselves . . . in what they are capable of.

Set within an extremely masculine world of power, both on the side of the authorities and the powerful and on that of community leaders, partisans, and trade unionists, Scorza's text deals with gender identities within this overall narrative scheme. Women appear in 'The Silent War' in the roles traditionally assigned to them within the Peruvian class structures: mothers, daughters, wives, prostitutes, young virgins, servants. Women are aware of and share in all the situations of loss and confrontation, always from within the structures of subordination . . . except for those who experience the vertigo of magic and the supernatural in their bodies.

Two women deserve mention: Doña Añada and Maca. I have already had the opportunity of commenting on Doña Añada elsewhere.[14] One extract will suffice here: 'This is the figure of the old woman Doña Añada, blind and humiliated by the haughty magistrate Montenegro, who turns her off the estate on which she has been in service all her life, on account of her old age. The community of Yanaconcha, to which the wise old woman belongs, takes her in, and she repays their hospitality by weaving and embroidering ponchos decorated with scenes from history. But, "in her blindness, Doña Añada had made mistakes. Instead of weaving, as she meant to, the disasters and triumphs of the past, she confected the disasters and triumphs to come" (Scorza, 1984: 124). By weaving threads she disobeyed and encouraged disobedience. The voice of Doña Añada's coloured threads rose up into a bulwark of possibility, of resistance: a feminine voice in which all possible authority was vested even though it came from the most powerless member of the community.'[15]

III. That we may be able to love men-women: Saint Maca, pray for us!

Now we come to Maca. Or Maco.

Man? Woman? Saint? Bandit? You tell me what s/he is....

No one knows. No one can be sure because Maca is what she wants to be, when s/he needs to be. Her ambiguous ambivalence has the saddest of stories, but then who does not have a sad story to tell?

The story of Maca/Maco runs through three of the novels: *Garabombo, el invisible*, *El cantar de Agapito Robles*, and *La tumba del relámpago*. She is born a girl, brought up in a family of gun-toting men, cattle-rustlers, and learns to ride and shoot like her brothers. Dressed as a boy, she has a better chance of survival in her family's precarious world. Once she has been thrown into prison, other men discover that the young robber has a woman's body and abuse her. So the violence done to the body of Maca/Maco is not that different from the violence done to all the occupied land, its dispossession. Maca goes on to learn to use this ambiguity in defence of her family, her marginal group, and herself.

In her appearances as woman and man, s/he arouses the most violent and beautiful passions in the whole of 'The Silent War'. Women fall passionately for Maco. Men become enamoured of Maca. When they discover the ambiguity of this seductive beauty they no longer know whether to call themselves men or women. Never mind! They just desire Maca/Maco ... in whichever guise s/he happens to appear. Women are desirous of the woman hidden in the man, men desirous of the man Maca also is. Set free from the desire they had learned, the men and women of 'The Silent War' discover that desire has many faces, takes many forms. At first frightened by the seductive ambiguity of Maca/Maco, men and women end up giving into desire as such.

Maca's sexual ambiguity also serves to disconcert the powerful. The consolidated structures of male and female are used to reproduce oppression and submission. Maca takes advantage of her ambiguous situation to confound the powerful and criticize the domesticated uses to which feminine sexuality is put in the service of men in positions of power. Don Migdonio, in the *Cantar de Agapito Robles*, proposes marriage to Maca – after a sex-filled night – in these words:

> 'My name is Migdonio de la Torre y Covarrubias del Campo del Moral. The de la Torres fought alongside Bolívar the Liberator in the campaign for independence. Our family has given the Republic one president, three generals, four bishops, and four speakers of the Supreme Court. Will you accept to become my wife?'
>
> Maca replies: 'I should rather accept three little *tamales* from you, if it is not offensive to be hungry after giving you so much to eat.'
>
> 'Little *tamales*?', the man asks.
>
> 'Yes, and green ones, unless your illustrious forebears have something against that colour.'

Don Migdonio proceeds to disgrace himself, to abandon his family and property, still without getting what he wants – Maca! Fr Chasan, in his confessional, never tires of hearing the people tell of their confused desires. Soon the story of Maca acquires accompaniments: miracles, healings, and salvations. Maca moves into the magical domain of goddesses and saints. Her ambiguity changes her into myth. Saints, men and women, are like this – a place in which people place their desires.

In *La tumba del relámpago*, Doroteo Silvestre comes to represent all the pain and fury of unlearning imposed desire till he reaches the point of freeing himself through desire that happens upon him. Doroteo sees Maca from afar during a bank robbery in which she, dressed as a woman, is crossing the square flirting and withdrawing. Their eyes meet for a second or less. Doroteo falls in love. When he asks who this woman is, he gets an unexpected answer: she is a man!

Impossible! Doroteo wants to deny the possibility that he – a man – has desired another man in full daylight . . . has let himself be confused by clothes and trinkets, by a man dressed as a woman! But Doroteo's body cannot forget the apparition. At first he tries to run away, to escape from the apparition and his desire. Then, beaten, in the middle of an erotic-religious experience of contemplation of the Virgin Mary, Doroteo decides to give in to the love that has happened to him and goes after Maca/Maco. Whatever will be . . .

The decision leaves Doroteo glowing. He cannot hide it; everyone sees his radiant body in the streets. . . . He tries to disguise it, to pass it off as an illness. But he knows: he is irradiated by this love that could not be – a man loving a man like that!

Doroteo gets close to Maco. Wherever s/he goes, s/he leaves unbelievable stories of impossible, unforgivable, unacceptable loves. But Doroteo keeps on, until he and Maco go down an alley where militiamen are facing them. The two are encircled. Doroteo fires, keeping his eyes on Maco/Maca – my love! The situation worsens. There is a rapid exchange of words, and Doroteo tells of his longstanding love. Maco smiles. Doroteo is distracted, and a bullet hits him. A stream of blood from his mouth turns into a flowering bougainvillea, whose exuberantly spreading branches help Maco flee from the militiamen.

This erotic ambiguity runs through the whole course of political and revolutionary struggle waged by the communities to liberate their land. It is not another story but the same one. Everything is mixed together, as it is in life. The men and women engaged in the struggle have their own stories, their bodily trajectories in which they also experience oppression. The struggle makes fantastic apparitions happen in their bodies too.

Reading 'The Silent War' brings to light different viewpoints on and different understandings of 'subjects', for both liberation theology and for practical efforts toward liberation. They are the poor as plural and complex events. Even in the analytical study of class, gender, ethnicity, and the like, the life of the poor as events of resistance and liberation spreads beyond set categories.

This plurality and ambiguity do not mean the dissolution of the historical subject but her/his total incarnation. Departing from the post-modern and bourgeois viewpoint of theologians intent on rejecting the centrality of the poor in theological and political discourse,[15] feminist and queer theologies are radically deepening the preferential option for the poor, in the knowledge that they can be what they like. Just as the sensual presence of the divine in starving and suffering bodies makes them glow, know what is yet to come, and become stronger, more beautiful, and more daring – to a degree they never thought themselves capable of.

Working alongside landless men and women in Brazil, I have more than once seen, or heard tell of, persons someone knows who have turned into an animal, become invisible, shown resistance . . . or of communities that have overcome hunger, of downtrodden women whom have turned into leaders, of men who have taken over the communal kitchen, of young people deciding to stay on the land, of the powerful being put down from their thrones, of the hungry being fed. . . . At such times, lit by the glow from the hearth as dawn was breaking over yet another day of land occupation, I have listened in wonder to the word – sometimes not knowing whether from the Bible or by Scorza – that keeps us living and happy one more time.

God with us.

Translated by Paul Burns

Notes

1. www.memorial.sp.gov.br/memorial/revistaNossa America/21/port/26-melhor_literatura.htm – 27k.
2. T. Pellegrini, review of *Literatura e Colonialismo, Rotas de navegação e comerçio no fantástico de Murilo Rubião*, in *Crítica Marxista* 16, São Paulo: Boitempo, p. 177.
3. M. Scorza, 1972, pp. 12–13, 29.
4. Camila Rodrigues, at http://www.historianet.com.br/conteudo/default.aspx?codigo=445 (Between 1862 and 1867 Napoleon III intervened militarily in Mexico with the aim of guaranteeing French commercial interests in America; it was at this time that the term 'Latin America' was coined); V. Romero, 'Du nominal "latin" pour l'Autre Amérique. Notes sur la naissance et le sens du nom "Amérique latine" autour des années 1850', at http://www.univ-paris-diderot.fr/hsal/hsal981/vr98-i.pdf.
5. Pelligrini, *loc. cit.*
6. C. Carvalhes, 'O pobre não tem sexo. A ausência dos discoursos de sexualidades na construção da noção de subjectividade na Teologia da Libertação', at http://www.margens.org.br'sis/revista3/artigos/tdl.pdf.
7. J. L. Segundo, *Libertação da Teologia*, São Paulo: Loyola, 1978.
8. http:/www2.fpa.org.br/portal/modules/news/article.php?storyid=1262.
9. G. García Márquez, *O amor e outros demônios*, Rio de Janeiro: Record, 1994, p. 113.
10. J. González Soto, 'La guerra silenciosa de Manuel Scorza: poesía crónica e parodia', at http://www.hispanista.co.br/revista/artigo04.htm.

11. J. C. Mariátegui, *Siete ensayos de interpretación de la realidad peruana*, Cali: Univ.del Valle, 1994.
12. Manuel Scorza, 'Literatura: el primer territorio libre de América', at http://64.233.169.104/search?q=cache:SUF-4QTRo_YJ:wwwlarepublica.co.pe/content/view'123047/28+%22manuel+scorza+%22&hl=pt-BR&ct=clnk&cd=27&gl=br.
13. González Soto, *loc. cit.*
14. N. Cardoso Pereira, 'Changing Seasons: About the Bible and other sacred texts in Latin America', in *Journal for the Study of the Old Testament / Feminist Interpretation of the Bible and the hermeneutics of Liberation*, London: Sheffield Academic Press, 2000, pp. 48–59.
15. J. M. Lorenzo Arribas, 'Discurso histórico y tradiciones críticas: Posibilidad del ecofeminismo y desobedencia', at http://www.antimilitaristas.org/article.php?id_article=2221.
16. A. C. de Melo Magalhâes, 'Teologia na Brasil nas décadas dos 70 e 80. Retrospectiva e propostas,' *Simpósio 47*, São Paulo: ASTE, 2005.

(D) 'A G-String is Not Samoan': Exploring a Transgressive Third-Gender Pasifika Theology

PHILIP CULBERTSON AND TAVITA MALIKO

The church defines people according to its theology of sin. Whatever you do, if you don't use your penis the way you are supposed to, then you are a homosexual. Whatever that means! (Tavita, interview 31 August 2007)

Introduction

Christian tradition has a long practice of gendering God. With certain exceptions (e.g., Julian of Norwich), God was gendered male until the rise of second-wave feminist theology (e.g., Mary Daly, Elizabeth Johnson, Phyllis Trible, Rosemary Ruether, Elisabeth Schüssler Fiorenza, Sallie McFague, Marcella Althaus Reid, and others), when feminine gendering began to be applied to God as one way to challenge the historically-conditioned grip of androcentrism and patriarchal metaphors.

Of course, gendered metaphors for the divine cannot capture the reality of God or the complexity of the divine-human relationship but can serve only to enrich the ways in which we think about who or what God might be. The best metaphors are those which break out of and deconstruct our compulsive anthropomorphism. However, if we must persist in gendering God, then new space for creative theologizing may be found by looking outside what Musa Dube calls 'Theology of The Empire'[1]—that is, to gendering as it is understood in traditional indigenous cultures. One such possibility lies in the gendered structuring of traditional Samoan culture.

I. The Third Gender of Polynesia

Samoa is an island nation in the South Pacific. It is believed that Samoans arrived in their islands approximately 3000 years ago from South-east Asia, and Samoan culture falls generally within that group of cultures sometimes called Polynesian. The French explorer Louis de Bougainville sighted the islands of Samoa in 1722, calling them the 'Navigator Islands'. Within forty years, European traders plying the Pacific started to call at Samoa for supplies, and a few Caucasians began to settle among the indigenous people. However, the greatest Western impact upon Samoans was caused by the arrival of Christian missionaries, particularly the London Missionary Society in 1830.

It is difficult to glean much information about indigenous Pacific cultures before the arrival of the European sailors and Christian missionaries. Scant records suggest that the White arrivals were surprised to discover males who played a recognizably feminine social role, including attempts to seduce the sailors.[2] And indeed, Samoan culture traditionally has cherished at least three genders.

The gender construction from which this essay is drawn is called, in Samoan, *fa'afafine*. While *-fafine* means 'woman', the causative prefix *fa'a-* is difficult to translate into English. The common English translation is 'like a woman,' though such translation is too literal accurately to describe the social role of *fa'afafine*. Anthropologist Douglass Drozdow-St.Christian defines as follows: 'The *fa'afafine* are genetically male in that they have penises. They use their penises in exactly the same way as males do: in heterosexual intercourse, urination, and in abiding by roles about modesty and exposure. However, the *fa'afafine* are not male, and their penises are not male sex organs. They are *fa'afafine* organs. That is, sex organs, but not ones which define the *fa'afafine* as male.'[3]

Sue Farran and Alexander Su'a define the term in a somewhat simpler way: 'people who, while of the male sex, might regard themselves and be regarded as, being of the feminine gender.'[4] For the sake of simplicity, we prefer to define *fa'afafine* as 'a human being with male genitals who, in terms of social gender-role, "leans toward a woman"'.

To understand this indigenous concept of multiple genders, one must accept Judith Butler's[5] argument that genitals determine biological sex, but do not then further determine gender or sexuality. In Butler's thinking, one 'performs' one's social gender-role – and by inference, one's sexuality –

independently of the genitals with which one is born. The severance of gender and sexuality from genitals allows, then, for a spectrum of ways in which these roles are performed in the social arena. Combining Butler's ideas with those of Robert Connell,[6] it can then be argued that in Samoan culture there are multiple masculinities, femininities, and *fa'afafini*ties. Indeed, most Pacific cultures include a third gender within their range of available social and sexual performances: the Tongan *fakafefine*, the Tahitian and Hawaiian *mahu*, the Fijian *vakasalewalewa*, the Maori *whakawahine*, the Cook Islands' *akava'ine*, and the *pinapinaaine* of Tuvalu and Kiribati.

II. Methodology

Philip is an American-born Caucasian middle-aged male who has worked in New Zealand for fifteen years as an academic. Tavita is a Samoan-born middle-aged male who has lived in New Zealand for ten years, and is a PhD candidate at the University of Auckland. Over the course of several years working together as academics, we have built a level of honesty and trust with each other, and we have written and published together before.[7] Yet our differences raise two problems in addressing the topic. The first is that neither of us is *fa'afafine*, and so we are speaking about people who carry identities significantly different from our own. Second, in writing this essay together, we are functioning as a cross-cultural research team. The literature of the social sciences, mental health, and practical theology highlights the problematics of cross-cultural research in terms of knowledges, power differentials, and assumptions. So to write together, we had to adopt some safety measures.

First, Philip, a non-Samoan, taped a two-hour interview with Tavita, a Samoan-born Samoan, and Tavita's opinions and experiences will be privileged in this essay. Second, Western anthropologists have written with some frequency about *fa'afafine* and the Samoan construction of gender, because third genders are an anthropological curiosity.[8] Much fine work has been produced by these anthropologists, which serves as an important resource for this essay. But *fa'afafine* must be allowed to speak for themselves in cross-cultural research, and when they do, it becomes obvious that not all anthropologists understand the experience of being *fa'afafine* in the same way. To address this discrepancy, we have also attempted in this research to cite the voices of *fa'afafine* as they appear in print media. Only in doing so can we begin to grasp how much 'a g-string is not Samoan'.

In the discipline of theology, little has been published about third gender constructions, including *fa'afafine*.⁹ This essay, then, is an attempt to explore the creative possibilities of thinking about God through the languaging and social behaviour—both of which are clearly metaphorical—of God as third-gendered.

III. *Fa'afafine* continued: the devil is in the details

The *fa'afafine* construction upon which this essay is built is assumed to be a part of the traditional Samoan social structure. By this logic, one would expect that the construct of *fa'afafine* would show up among the pantheon of indigenous Samoan gods and goddesses, as described in traditional mythology. Evidence, however, is not clear. There is a Samoan myth about Pili, son of the creator god Tagalaolagi. This Pili coupled with Sinaletavae, and they had four children. Residents of the small Samoan islands of Apolima and Manono understand that these four children were males. Variations on the myth, however, claim that three of these children were males and that the fourth, Tolufale, was *fa'afafine*.¹⁰

Traditionally, children begin to be trained in culturally-defined gender-roles around the age of twelve. The freedom of childhood becomes restricted around this time. Based on their biological sex, boundaries are set around various gender performances, through parental instructions about gendered behaviour. Some families 'recognize' their *fa'afafine* children, as such, around the age of puberty or early teen-age, but at least one *fa'afafine* claims that by the age of four, s/he was recognizable as *fa'afafine*, even replacing her given name of Tafi with a chosen name of Alicia.¹¹ The etiology of *fa'afafine* identity is not clear. Since 'work' is highly gendered in Samoan culture, some writers claim that a *fa'afafine* is 'recruited' within families that have too many boys, and not enough girls to perform the tasks which are culturally assigned to women.¹² This argument does not easily account for families in which there are four, or even more, *fa'afafine* in one generation, especially when 'recruitment' would leave a family with too few boys to accomplished the gendered labour. The self-stories of *fa'afafine* we were able to locate seem to claim that *fa'afafine* generally understand themselves as 'born that way'.¹³

Within the family, *fa'afafine* generally 'lean toward' those tasks of family-maintenance that are traditionally assigned to females, such as food preparation, weaving and cloth-making, and the care of the young and the elderly.

Yet, 'fa'afafine are viewed by their *aiga* [families] as sons or brothers, not daughters or sisters. They have the freedom to roam about and go beyond the village that males rather than females have. At the same time they may be permitted to work with their sisters and even to share the same sleeping accommodation because they are not perceived as being a sexual threat. . . . [S]ome village councils recognize the *fa'afafine* preferences for women's activities to those of men, and may or may not allow them to wear female clothing in the village.[14] A *fa'afafine*, although genetically male, can also perform the role of the *taupou*, the symbolic and ritualized 'virgin female' of the village.[15]

Some *fa'afafine* eventually marry women and sire children;[16] others do not. Some *fa'afafine* wear clothes that signal masculinity; others wear clothes that signal femininity.[17] Some prefer heterosexual sex and marriage, an esteemed relational status due to the high value placed on producing succeeding generations of large families;[18] others prefer sex with both biological males and biological females.[19] Some prefer sex only with biological males, though this is not to be considered as concurrent with Western definitions of 'homosexuality', for sex between a male and a *fa'afafine* is viewed as sex between a male and a non-male.[20]

In general, *fa'afafine* are most visible publicly between adolescence and their mid-thirties. After that, some will have married, and more recently, others will have emigrated away from Samoa. There is very little evidence available about the lives of older *fa'afafine*. Tavita cannot remember seeing any during his time living in Samoa, and we could only find two relevant print references.[21]

IV. *Fa'afafine* and the measures of masculinity

Traditionally in Samoan culture, the social spheres of young men and women are held quite far apart, once they are past about the age of eight. In Western cultures, where there is a (generally uncreative) binary opposition of male and female, masculinity is often measured by its 'distance' from anything which smacks of femininity. But how does this work in a culture with three genders?

> **Tavita:** Children call each other names, and I was called a *fa'afafine* – thankfully not by other children, but by my own immediate family – because at the age of four I complained about having to pick up something

which was too heavy for me. These are the wounds I still carry around within me which perhaps shaped my relationship to women, especially to gay men, to a very large extent. Because I hated being labeled a *fa'afafine*, I learned to be as far away from that kind of person as possible, disallowing any possible intimate relationship with men in general.

In other words, growing up as an adolescent male in Samoa, Tavita learned to 'measure his masculinity' by the distance of his own gender-performances from those of a *fa'afafine*, rather than from the gender-performances of females.

More recently, this measure was again confirmed for Tavita. His brother-in-law, who is *fa'afafine*, currently works as a lecturer in Performing Arts at a Pacific university.

> **Tavita:** I got married more than fifteen years ago. When I was introduced to my wife's family, I noticed that her youngest brother is a *fa'afafine*. The mother was always coming to his defence because the father, as soon as his *fa'afafine* son would come into his sight, would swear at him, calling him a 'fucking *fa'afafine*.' But this son grew up and now does well for himself, and now he has a traditional man's tattoo [*pe'a*, a waist-to-knee, complicated tattoo in carefully-regulated motifs]. Getting that tattoo seems to have confirmed to his father that now his son is a real man. That's a confirmation to the public – No, my son is a male.

Once Tavita's brother-in-law had inscribed upon his body the traditional Samoan tattoo which signals masculinity, and had achieved acclaim in his chosen professional world, his father appears to have no longer viewed him as a *fa'afafine*, but as a culturally-sanctioned Samoan male.

V. Varieties of *fa'afafine* over time and space

Just as in Butler's terms we understand the variety of ways in which both masculinity and femininity are performed, so there are many variations in which the gender-role of *fa'afafine* is performed. Drozdow-St.Christian writes: '... drag-defined *fa'afafine* are distinguishable from other *fa'afafine* by Samoans themselves. There are street *fa'afafine*, the business *fa'afafine*, the back village traditional *fa'afafine*, the homosexual men. Finer and finer distinctions are being drawn. Gender absolutism, the investing of the invisible with the power to foreclose meaning prior to meaning itself, as accompanied the repressive tendencies of Christianization and the invention of what many Samoans describe as modern sensibilities.[22]

There are married *fa'afafine* and unmarried, urban and rural, Samoan-born and New Zealand-born, younger and older, and *fa'afafine* migrants from Samoa to Auckland, Sydney, Los Angeles, Detroit, and even Alaska.[23] Globalization and the restless tide of migration are impacting upon the gender performance and identity of *fa'afafine*. Natural and inevitable as this may be, some Samoans see the breakdown of the gender-fluidity of their traditional culture as being a threat:

> **Tavita:** My brother-in-law is popular as a performer in the Pacific countries. For him to come across as a *real* Samoan performer, his tattoo is more affirming of his status as a man, as a male entertainer.
> **Philip:** So if he has a *pe'a*, he can't wear a g-string and a short skirt?
> **Tavita:** Oh, he does wear g-strings. I've got one of her performances on a DVD, and in one of the skits, he came onto the stage in a g-string. Mind you, it's like a – because he has a g-string and a *pe'a*, that's quite different from wearing a g-string without a *pe'a*. In either case, you're almost naked, but of course, with a *pe'a* you are considered to be clothed.
> **Philip:** But doesn't the juxtaposition of g-string on top of a *pe'a* look a bit odd to a Pacific audience?
> **Tavita:** It was to me! I would have thought it would have been better to cover up the g-string – not because I don't like the g-string, but because the g-string brought out a Western element of him as an entertainer. If he had tried to come up with a few flowers, so I could see if he is covered up – even if the g-string was in the form of flowers, that's better than – because a g-string is not Samoan. So for me as part of the audience, it was disturbing.
> **Philip:** Do you think he did it for that reason, to disturb?
> **Tavita:** I don't know. I'll ask him!

It is not his brother-in-law's gender performance as a *fa'afafine*, or his near-nudity on stage that offends Tavita. It is, rather, the juxtaposition of a Western garment, with sexual overtones, on top of a traditional symbol of masculinity and honour, however over-determined, that offends Tavita's sensibility as a middle-aged Samoan of chiefly rank. 'A g-string is not Samoan.' This simple statement sums up the anxiety of traditional Pacific cultures over the changes in their cultural heritage that globalization threatens.

VI. Evangelical missionaries and the *fa'afafine*

When the London Missionary Society arrived in Samoa in 1840, it brought a form of Victorian evangelical Christianity that quickly took root in the islands. Within that missionary heritage lay an unconscious attempt to impose the Western dichotomous opposition of two genders upon the indigenous structure of three genders. As well, it was apparently part of the missionary strategy to replace the traditional authority of the *matai* (chiefs) with the authority of the local minister, thereby giving the minister the power to 'divide' families, should they wish, by excluding *fa'afafine* from attending worship. Some local churches made such an exclusion, and others did not, so that today, there is no consistent pattern across the Samoan Churches both in Samoa and overseas.[24] There are, however, to the best of our knowledge, no *fa'afafine* in ordained positions in congregations in Samoa.

Fa'afafine do participate in local congregations often, however.

> **Tavita**: In our church, there is a *fa'afafine* who is the choral conductor. Last Sunday I was preaching, and as I sat in the pulpit looking at the choir before the service, I heard this very high soprano from amongst the group of sopranos. As I looked, it was the *fa'afafine*, the conductor, sitting right up in the front among the young girls, and he is singing at the top of his voice, above every other of the young female sopranos. Now, he is accepted.
> **Philip**: How old is he?
> **Tavita**: At least thirty, but under forty. But he will come to church dressed like a man, in a shirt, and a tie and a *lavalava*, and like that.
> **Philip**: Does everyone in the congregation know he is a *fa'afafine*?
> **Tavita**: I think so.

Farran and Su'a also emphasize the important roles that *fa'afafine* play in local congregations: '*Fa'afafine* are . . . often valuable members of the church, singing in choirs and participating in fund-raising, acting as deacons, Sunday-school teachers, church youth leaders and participating in many church activities. They may even attend church dressed in frocks or Samoan *puletasi*. Yet many churches appear to be ambiguous about *fa'afafine*, who may be subject to verbal castigation from the pulpit and from church members.[25]

Tavita senses that these levels of discrimination against *fa'afafine* in the Church are increasing, due to the rising influence of certain forms of conservative evangelical Christianity imported from overseas. In some churches, ministers are teaching their congregations that the correct English translation for *fa'afafine* is 'homosexual,' and that the assumed 'sins' of Sodom and Gomorrah included being *fa'afafine*.

Of course, the Bible has very little vocabulary for the ways in which we discuss gender and sexuality following Butler's views. Yet we find it surprising that Samoan clergy, almost all of whom are Samoan-born and Samoan-trained, could confuse the traditional cultural structures of gender performance with a dualistic essentialist dialogue about sexuality. By falling prey to such confusion, the Samoan clergy themselves become the re-colonizers of their own people, in the process threatening to destroy Samoa's indigenous family structures, wisdom, and spirituality. In general, open resistance to Western Christianity's assumptions and exegeses is rare in Samoa, but this example seems particularly tragic to us.

VII. Exploring a transgressive *Fa'afafine* theology

If we could push further apart the gendered metaphors we ordinarily use for God, what might we find in 'the marginalized centre'? What could we understand of God if we spoke metaphorically of the Divine *Fa'afafine* who inhabits liminal spaces, rather than of Father Lord and Mother God? In order to explore this new space, we would have to refuse those metaphors for God that imply divine genitals, and instead focus on gender performance within covenantal relationships. We would, instead, need to conceptualize God's gender performance as 'transgressive'.

The Divine *Fa'afafine* can roam with the boys outside the boundaries of the village, the familiar spaces of safety and security, and yet can find rest and refreshment in the spaces where women sleep. The Divine *Fa'afafine* could appear in men's clothing or women's clothing, depending on mood or whim, and we would be just fine with that. The Divine *Fa'afafine* could pound the *kava* to refresh our spirits, and weave beautiful *tapa* cloths in which we could bury our dead. The Divine *Fa'afafine* would find particular pleasure in pursuits such as music and dancing, service to others, and education that focuses on both tradition and the future. Like a *pe'a*, or traditional Samoan tattoo, we could ask that God's body be inscribed on our own theologies and devotions. The Divine *Fa'afafine* would haunt our churches, singing soprano in the choir in her *puletasi*, and moving the furniture in his *lavalava*, yet also being regularly abused from the pulpit, as our human and cultural prejudices and expectations are hurled her way.

And ultimately, perhaps the Divine *Fa'afafine* would seek a consort. In the heavens, where boundaries are broken and margins privileged, perhaps s/he would meet The Manly-Hearted Woman, or Ninawaki, who, according to the Blackfeet tribes, loves politics, tells dirty jokes, and owns horses.[26] And then, all manner of things shall be well.

Notes

1. Musa Dube, *Postcolonial Feminist Interpretation of the Bible*, Nashville: Christian Board of Publication, 2000.
2. See Nico Besnier, 'Polynesian Gender Liminality through Time and Space,' in Gilbert Herdt (ed), *Third Sex, Third Gender*, New York: Zone Books, 2006, pp. 288–92; Kerry James, 'Effeminate males and changes in the construction of gender in Tonga,' *Pacific Studies*, 17, 1994, pp. 39–40; and G. Mortimer, *Observations and remarks made during a voyage* (1791).
3. Douglass Drozdow-St. Christian, *Elusive Fragments: Making Power, Propriety & Health in Samoa*, Durham, NC: Carolina Academic Press, 2002, p. 96.
4. Sue Farran and Alexander Su'a, 'Discriminating on the Grounds of Status: Criminal Law and *Fa'afafine* and *Fakaleiti* in the South Pacific,' *Journal of South Pacific Law* (2005), IX:1, at http://www.paclii.org/journals/fJSPL/vol09no1/5.shtml., 2005, p. 1.
5. Judith Butler, *Undoing Gender*, New York: Routledge, 2004.
6. Robert Connell, *Masculinities*, New York: Polity Press, ^{2}2005.
7. In Philip Culbertson, Margaret Nelson Agee, and Cabrini 'Ofa Makasiale, eds., *Penina Uliuli: Contemporary Challenges in Mental Health for Pacific Peoples*, Honolulu: University of Hawai'i Press, 2007.
8. M. Morgan Holmes, 'Locating Third Sexes,' *Transformations* (July 2004), *VIII*, 1–14, at http://www.transformationsjournal.org/journal/issue_08/article_03.shtml; Rosalind Morris, 'All Made Up: Performance Theory and the New Anthropology of Sex and Gender,' *Annual Review of Anthropology*, XXIVI, 1995, pp. 567–92
9. An exception is Marcella Althaus-Reid, *The Queer God*, New York: Routledge, 2003.
10. Samoan Prime Minister Tuilaepa Sailele Malielegaoi, in Terry Tavita, 'Faafafine are Useful People, says PM,' *Savali Newspaper* (27 July 2006) at http://www.govt.ws/sv_article.cfm?sv_id=260.
11. Julie O'Malley, 'Born a boy in Samoa, living as a woman in Alaska,' at *Pop Matters*, http://www.popmatters.com/pm/news/article/47598/born-a-boy-

in-samoa-living-as-a-woman-in-alaska/, 23 August 2007, p. 3.
12. Sue Farran, 'Transsexuals, *Fa'afafine, Fakaleiti* and Marriage Law in the Pacific: Considerations for the Future,' *Journal of the Polynesian Society* (2004) CXIII:2, 120; Australian Broadcasting Corporation, 'Fa'afafine—Samoan boys brought up as girls,' at http://www.abc.net.au/ra/pacific/people/hazy.htm.
13. Samoan Prime Minister Tuilaepa Sailele Malielegaoi argues 'and if the blind and the fa'afafine are born that way, then did not God create them that way? And should not we all accept and respect all of God's creations as they were fashioned in His image?' Terry Tavita, 'Faafafine are Useful People . . .'
14. Farran and Su'a, p. 7.
15. Ibid.
16. Drozdow-St Christian, pp. 30, 155; Farran, p. 138. We disagree with the arguments of Tamasailau Sua'ali'i ('Samoans and Gender: Some Reflections on Male, Female, and Fa'afafine Gender Identities,' in *Tangata O Te Moana Nui*, Palmerston North: Dunmore Press, 2001, p. 170) who argues that *fa'afafine* are able to sire children only via medical intervention.
17. Holmes, p. 7, rejects the use of 'transgender' or 'cross-dresser' for describing *fa'afafine*, as does Nico Besnier, 'Polynesian Gender Liminality in Time and Space.'
18. Farran, p. 138.
19. Drozdow-St Christian, p. 155.
20. O'Malley, p. 2. *Fa'afafine* Alicia understands herself as a straight woman who is attracted to straight men.
21. Australian Broadcasting Corporation, 'Fa'afafine—Samoan boys brought up as girls,' which references an older *fa'afafine* named 'Hazy'; and 'Growing divide between Central and South Auckland 'third sex' communities,' *Express*, 12 September 2007, p. 4, which references older *fa'afafine* living in South Auckland, New Zealand.
22. Drozdow-St Christian, pp. 32–33.
23. Farran & Su'a, p. 2, Farran pp. 121, 137, O'Malley.
24. According to Farran and Su'a, p. 6, 'There is also a distinction between those churches which have become integrated into the *fa'asamoa*, and those churches which arrived later and follow a more westernized approach which at times is in conflict with traditional Samoan ways. In the former there may be greater acceptance of *fa'afafine* as part of the *fa'asamoa*, although this is by no means uniform.'
25. Farran and Su'a, p. 5.
26. Alison Shaw and Shirley Ardener, eds., *Changing Sex and Bending Gender*, Oxford: Berghahn Books, 2005.

Unfixing Nature: Homosexuality and Innovating Natural Law

ERIC BORGMAN

At the end of October 2007, there was a controversy in Italy about a poster protesting against discrimination of homosexuals. On the poster was a photograph with a baby, wearing a bracelet with the word 'homosexual' on it.

It was one of the many instances in which it is revealed that there is a struggle going on between two natures. One nature functions as guarantee of what is considered to be normal behaviour. The statement is made with different degrees of sophistication, but it comes down to: it is natural for human beings to be sexually attracted to people of the opposite sex. Here, nature is generic and functions as an allegedly objective norm. There are people feeling and acting differently, but what they do is against nature. The remedy for them is to submit to and reconnect with true nature. The other nature is personalized and subjective. The argument here also comes in different degrees of sophistication, but it comes down to: for me as a woman it is my nature to be attracted to women or for me as a man it is my nature to be attracted to men. Here, nature also functions as a norm. If this is my nature – or, in a religious variation, if God has made me this way – and it does not harm anyone, it is my right or even my duty to behave accordingly. Thus, homosexuality is seen as natural by some and as against nature by others. One party is fanatically trying to show that the other party is wrong in thinking that homosexuality is biologically founded. The other party in turn is trying to show that the first party is in fact homophobic and use arguments that seem scientific, but are in fact ideological.

A few years ago, as part of a controversy over his book on gender-bending and transsexualism, the psychologist and sex researcher J. Michael Bailey claimed that identity politics is 'a hindrance to scientific truth'.[1] In his view, the experience many transsexuals witness to, that they always have felt females locked up in a male body and that therefore nature made a mistake that was mended by their sex change operation, is illusionary. Here I do not want to discuss Bailey's highly controversial claim that transsexualism is either extreme homosexuality or 'autogynephilia', the tendency to be sexually aroused by the thought or image of yourself as a woman.[2] Here I am concerned with the apparent authority of arguments from nature in matters of sexuality in this debate. Bailey does think that homosexuality is something one is born with, as a result of hereditary and prenatal influences. Therefore it should be accepted and taken for granted. At the same time, he suggests that transsexualism has a psychological origin and therefore can and should be changed. In Bailey's view, anybody who does not want to see this is in fact clinging to the illusionary certainty of a biologically-founded sexual identity, blocking further scientific research on how sexual identity is formed.

What Bailey does not seem to recognize, however, is the point I want to make here. The mere existence of identity politics challenges all essentialist ideas of sexual orientation. Apparently, there is an important socio-cultural element present in what one experiences as one's identity, sexually or otherwise. Nature functions in the debates on sexual identity as an important source of authority. I will argue in this article that the Catholic 'natural law' tradition offers a way to think differently about sexuality. Its conception of nature includes culture, directionality toward the good life, and openness to unexpected possibilities for a God-given future. Unfortunately, the Catholic 'natural law' tradition in its official ecclesial form took over the modern ideas of 'nature' as static common norm, somehow visible in the way things are going and working in what is considered as nature. This 'biologization' of nature in dominant theologies has led, in the 1980s, to a theology that claims to be 'counter-natural'. In line with aspects of liberation theology and with Karl Barth's resistance to 'natural theology', and suspecting that what is supposed to be natural is in fact the status quo projected on to nature, homosexuality was claimed as an important issue in the counter-cultural struggle for liberation.[3] Indeed, what is labelled as homosexuality ultimately challenges the very idea of a fixed 'nature', in human beings at least.[4] In order to spell out the theological implications of this, I think it is important to develop an alternative view on a non-fixed nature of which we are active parts. That is what I set out to do in this article by revisiting the 'natural law' tradition.

I. Homosexuality and the openness of sexual acts to procreation

According to the official doctrine of the hierarchy of the Roman Catholic Church, 'homosexual acts are intrinsically disordered and can in no case be approved of'. They 'lack an essential and indispensable finality', because they do not 'preserve the full sense of mutual self-giving and human procreation in the context of true love.'[5] It is never explicitly said that homosexual partners cannot truly love one another. And what is more, the documents make clear that people with a homosexual inclination that is definitive because of 'some kind of innate instinct or a pathological constitution judged to be incurable', should be respected and not 'unjustly discriminated' against – leaving open what 'unjustly' means here. But the final conclusion is that homosexuals act are 'contrary to the natural law' because they 'close the sexual act to the gift of life' and 'do not proceed from a genuine affective and sexual complementarity', which can only exist between male and female. This in fact comes quite close to the claim that homosexual love can never be true love.[6]

It is rather obvious that sexual acts between persons of the same sex are not directed toward receiving the 'gift of life', i.e. the conception of a child. But it is important to look somewhat closer at the demand that every single sexual act should be open to this gift because it is intrinsically directed to it. It was *Humanae vitae* in 1968 that first stated that every single sexual act has to be directed toward the conception of new life because that is its objective nature, still strongly stressed in official Catholic teaching. This contrasts with the teaching of Vatican II, where the mission of married couples is much more broadly formulated: it is 'to transmit human life and to educate their children; they should realize that they are thereby cooperating with the love of God the Creator and are, in a certain sense, its interpreters'. It is their responsibility to discover what that means concretely in their circumstances of time and place, although they should realize that 'in their behaviour they may not simply follow their own fancy, but must be ruled by conscience – and conscience ought to be conformed to the law of God in the light of the teaching authority of the Church'.[7] Without the positive statements from the hierarchical Church, one could make a case in favour of child adoption by homosexual married couples from this just as easily as a case against the use of contraceptives.

Already in *Humanae vitae* the focus shifts from cooperating with the creative love of God to humbly and reverentially receiving new life as a gift and a responsibility from God. In the encyclical, Paul VI declares that 'the fundamental nature of the marriage act' – church jargon for sexual intercourse – 'while uniting husband and wife in the closest intimacy, also renders them capable of generating new life—and this as a result of laws written into the actual nature of man and of woman'. This 'inseparable connection, established by God . . . between the unitive significance and the procreative significance which are both inherent to the marriage act', should be respected and may not be broken by human beings 'on their own initiative'. There is a deep awe for the mystery of the generation of new life, in which *Humanae vitae* sees almost directly the expression of God's power as creator: 'Just as man does not have unlimited dominion over his body in general, so also, and with more particular reason, he has no such dominion over his specifically sexual faculties, for these are concerned by their very nature with the generation of life, of which God is the source'.[8] Thus, the general statement that the 'transmission of human life is a most serious role in which married people collaborate freely and responsibly with God the Creator', with which the encyclical starts, leads to the conclusion that 'each and every marital act must of necessity retain its intrinsic relationship to the procreation of human life', as an expression of the awareness of a couple that their marriage 'takes its origin from God, who 'is love' (1 John 4.8), the Father 'from whom every family in heaven and on earth is named' (Eph. 3.15)'.[9]

II. Human capacity to procreate an expression of God's creative power?

This is not 'biologism' in the strict sense. It is not that only the biological aspect of sexual behaviour is considered and the human activity of giving meaning to sexuality is ignored.[10] But it is biologism in a deeper sense, or even 'bio-theology' if one would want to call it that. The biological reality of sex leading to procreation is itself directly and heavily invested with religious meaning. Thus human involvement in correcting and changing what is commonly considered to be 'nature' or 'natural' – which is in fact an aspect of almost all cultural activity and is theologically based on the idea that the nature we live in and are part of is not the world God created and called 'very good' (Gen. 1.31) but is in the process of becoming that world (which leads for instance to the acceptance of medicine) – can, where sexual matters are concerned, only be viewed as breaking the connection between sexual intimacy and the gift of life, which is in itself holy.

John Paul II, who was already concerned with the issue of sexuality and marriage when he was still archbishop Karol Wojtyla of Krakow, and who was involved in the drafting process of *Humanae vitae*, made this religious reading of biological facts and characteristics into the starting point of an unprecedented philosophico-theological system.[11] In September 1979 he started a series of, in total, 130 addresses at the general audiences in the Vatican, in which he developed a systematic 'Theology of the Body'.[12] In his view the essence of being human was to express love in a bodily relation of mutual self-giving between a man and a woman, directed toward fertility as openness toward God's gift of new life. According to John Paul II 'the procreative capacity, inscribed in human sexuality, is – in its deepest truth – a cooperation with God's creative power'. In this view it is not in the first place by responsibly shaping their sexuality according to God's will with the world as revealed in the message and the life, death, and resurrection of Jesus the Anointed One, but by submitting to the undisturbed internal mechanisms of human fertility that sexual partners sanctify their lives.[13]

III. The tradition of natural law

No sophisticated ideological critique is needed to reveal the heterosexual bias in this analysis of human sexuality. This direct theological reading of the biological facts of heterosexual intercourse as immediately expressing the will of God makes it impossible even to consider the possibility that sexual intimacy of people of the same sex might be a valuable expression of human love. The view of nature developed here, however, is much more in line with eighteenth- and nineteenth-century versions of 'Physico-Theology' than with the Catholic tradition of thinking in terms of natural law and natural theology.[14] Physico-Theology saw God behind the miraculous, awe-inspiring harmony of the natural universe. In fact it identified both so intimately that this harmony itself was seen as the presence of the divine in the world. The teaching of the hierarchical Church of God's presence in the physical mechanisms of conception, pregnancy, and procreation share with it the tendency to make nature as it is known and understood at a certain moment in history the direct expression of God's will.

This is not the case in the much older tradition of thinking in terms of 'natural law'. In the Aristotelian and Thomistic tradition, the most important aspect of 'nature' is that it has directionality. Everything that is, has the natural tendency to fulfil its purpose. While it is the purpose of an acorn to grow into an oak, it is the purpose of human beings to become happy by searching and realizing the common good, which is also a relationship with God as the One who is true Goodness in him- or herself. Human beings are created not to stay as they are, but to realize their true happiness. Nature – nature as aspect of human existence, but also nature as the lives of animals and plants and the existence of lifeless nature – is good as far as it contributes to this happiness in an all-encompassing community. However, it is also the other way round: true happiness is in harmony with what nature, which is a gift from the same God that is the end of the striving for happiness, enables and allows. What violates the body, but also what works counter to the sustainability of the earth, cannot be the true happiness that is the end of our God-created lives.[15] For human beings, this end should be striven for in freedom. Therefore, in matters concerning human morality the 'natural law' is the law of practical reason and the law of human virtue.[16]

That the fullness of God's goodness as a transcendent goal of life is in harmony with the immanent needs of human beings, animals, plants, and – if it makes sense to speak of 'needs' there – lifeless nature: that is the fundamental claim of the theological tradition of thinking in terms of 'natural law'. Therefore it is not sacrilegious to experience and to think of good cooking and good lovemaking as sacramental representations – signs and instruments – of the ultimate happiness that is the end of human existence. This implies that nature cannot be treated as simply instrumental to any human project claiming to realize true happiness, but represents a value in itself. But it also implies that no mechanism or aspect of nature can in itself be seen as direct expression of God's power. Nature as it is is as little nature as it is meant to be to let God be all in all, as society as it is is society as it is meant to be to represent God's reign on earth.[17]

IV. Exploring new possibilities as contributions to the good life

This makes sexual desire the expression of the natural human urge to bond together, to fulfil each other's longings, to enjoy each other's company and to enjoy being enjoyed as each other's company and each other's fulfilment. From this perspective, no specific forms of sexual behaviour are in themselves natural or counter-natural, just as there are no natural or counter-natural ways of eating or moving. No uses of sexual organs are natural or counter-natural, and being inventive in this respect is no more sinful than being inventive in cooking or dancing. No sexual behaviour has to be excused. If it builds enduring and humanizing bonds of mutual obligation and respect in which *eros* becomes an expression of *agape*, it contributes to the diversity of goodness and of being good that will be integrated in the fullness of life that is the end of our common existence as human beings in community with the rest of creation. Exploring a true gay or lesbian life in all its aspects, or another sexual identity that does not have a name but that one is called to develop, breaking down barriers and discovering new and liberating possibilities, can be a valuable contribution to humanity, and thus to the community of the Church. It realizes possibilities of being good and true that have previously been undiscovered.[18] It is not because it cannot be helped that we should accept homosexuality, as it so often seems in even supposedly 'progressive' theological views. It is because it opens up new possibilities of expressing and cultivating the good life that were hidden and repressed, but which contribute to the fullness of happiness that is the future of human beings in God. And it is to the degree that they do so that they should not just be accepted and tolerated but should be considered as valuable in themselves for religious and theological reasons.

'The Church needs to do more thinking about sex', is the last sentence of a book on 'sex and Catholicism' from the British theologian and Dominican Gareth Moore.[19] This claim is rather counter-intuitive. According to many of our contemporaries, Catholics and others, the Church thinks way too much about sex. It has become almost a commonplace that if theology and the Church would stop interfering with sex and sexual behaviour, their problems would automatically disappear. Is seems, however, that Moore is right. The hierarchical Church, and its theology, *talk* a lot about sex and declare firmly and unequivocally what they think to be right and wrong. But this means in fact that it avoids *thinking* about sex. Sex, like all human behaviour, is not first of all about rules and regulations, but about cultivating life, by developing and sustaining a particular culture as a complex system of ways of conduct and reflection on these ways of conduct. The critical question is whether a culture, in general and in its different aspects, serves the life-giving God of which biblical and Christian traditions speak and contributes to a perspective in which this God is the future of all human beings, superabundantly fulfilling their longing and natural striving for happiness. The reflections on 'natural law' that I presented in this article do therefore not lead to a variation of bio-theology, but to a theology of culture as a theology directed to fulfilling and cultivating the world as God's creation.[20]

This takes seriously the Christian confession of the incarnation and the *kenosis* of God in Jesus Christ. God is present among us with unprecedented bodily intimacy, not only in awe-inspiring mechanisms of procreation but also in our most elementary desires and the humblest, often not very glorious acts of sexual love-making. God is present there as the mystery that gives us, in and through our human shaping and reshaping of the world in all its aspects, including ourselves, a future of unimagined and unimaginable happiness. The author of St John's Apocalypse (or Revelation) speaks of a new heaven and a new earth: 'the first heaven and the first earth has passed away' (Rev. 21.1). Nature as it is, and our current imagination of what it means, what it allows, and what it enables cannot define the limits of what will be. Not socially, but also not sexually. At the same time, this cultural-theological approach of sexuality takes seriously that there is sexual behaviour that is wrong and even evil: egotistical, violent, humiliating, degrading, dehumanizing. This clearly does not contribute to the fullness of happiness and should be avoided. The law, however, that distinguishes between what is right and what is wrong in matters of sexuality is a law that is not simply present and clearly accessible. It is not by reading the working of our sexual organs that we can discover what to do and what to avoid. What is good has to be sought in human nature and its directionality, but it has to reveal itself time and again in the new future that this directionality seeks and God gives: 'Teach me, my God, the way of your statutes, and I will keep it to the end' (Psalm 119: 33).

Notes

1. J. M. Bailey, *The Man Who Would Be Queen: The Science of Gender-Bending and Transsexualism*, Washington D.C.: Joseph Henri Press, 2003. Cf. <http://www.iasr.org/meeting/2003/abstracts2003.pdf>
2. Cf. for a history R. Blanchard, 'The Origin of the Concept of Autogynephilia', at <http://www.autogynephilia.org/origins.htm> For the controversy, cf. Y. L. S. Smith, St. van Goozen, A. J. Kupier, P. T. Cohen-Kettenis, 'Transsexual subtypes: Clinical and theoretical significance', *Psychiatry Research* 137 (2005) 151–160. Also controversial, however, is Bailey's ethical behaviour as a researcher and the scientific quality – or its absence – of his book.
3. See G. Ménard, *De Sodome à l'Exode: Jalons pour une théologie de la libération gaie*, Montréal, 1980; R. Reeling Brouwer and F. J. Hirs, *De verlossing van ons lichaam: Tegen natuurl_ke theologie*, 's Gravenhage: Boekencentrum, 1985. (Ger. trans. *Die Erlösung unseres Leibes: Schwul-theologische Überlegungen wider natürliche Theologie*, Joseph Wittingen: Erev-Rav, 1995).

Unfixing Nature   81

4. Cf. M. Althaus-Reid, *Indecent Theology: Theological Perversions in Sex, Gender and Politics*, London: Routledge, 2000; *idem, The Queer God*, London: Routledge, 2003; *idem, The Sexual Theologian: Essays on Sex, God and Politics*, London: T. & T. Clark, 2004.
5. Congregation for the Doctrine of Faith, 'Declaration on certain Questions Concerning Sexual Ethics *Persona humana*' (29 Dec. 1975), no. 8 and 5; cf. Vatican II, 'Pastoral Constitution on the Church in the Modern World *Gaudium et spes*' (7 Dec. 1965), no. 49 and 51.
6. *Catechism of the Catholic Church* (11 Oct. 1992), no. 2357.
7. *Gaudium et spes*, l.c., no. 50.
8. Paul VI, encyclical *Humanae vitae* (25 July 1968), no. 12 and 13.
9. *Ibid.* no. 1 and 11. Here, the encyclical quotes Pius XI, encyclical *Casti connubi* (31 Dec. 1930) and Pius XII, Address to the Congress of the Italian Catholic Association of Midwives (29 Oct. 1951).
10. This is often – wrongly – suggested by critics of *Humanae vitae*; cf. J. E. Smith, *Humanae Vitae: A Generation Later*, Washington DC: The Catholic University of America Press, 1991, pp. 68–128.
11. See already his *Love and Responsibility*, London & New York: William Collins/Farrar, Straus and Giroux, 1981 (trans. from Polish original, 1960). For Wojtyla's relation to *Humanae vitae* at the time of its writing, cf. G. Weigel, *Witness to Hope: The Biography of Pope John Paul II*, New York: HarperCollins, 1999, pp. 206–10.
12. It would eventually lead to the publication of John Paul II, *The Theology of the Body: Human Life in the Divine Plan*, Boston, Mass.: Pauline Books and Media, 1997. For the background and the plan of the addresses as publicly presenting an alternative to modern Western visions of sexuality, cf. Weigel, *Witness to Hope*, pp. 333–43. For a summary of the views of Wojtyla/John Paul II on marriage and sexuality, cf. Smith, *Humanae vitae*, pp. 230–65.
13. This is also the reason why family planning by making use of the 'natural' period of infertility of the women is presented as permitted and why marriage does not lose its value when remaining infertile for 'natural' reasons. Cf. also John Paul II, Apostolic Exhortation on the Role of the Christian Family in the Modern World *Familiaris consortio* (22 Nov. 1981) no. 32.
14. I am close to much of the criticism by Charles Curran here on the 'physicalism' and the static 'classicism' of *Humanae vitae* and the subsequent official teaching on sexuality, but I disagree with his suggestion that this makes the natural-law tradition obsolete; cf. C. E. Curran, *Contraception, Authority and Dissent*, New York: Herder and Herder, 1969; *idem* and R. E. Hunt, *Dissent in and for the Church: Theologians and Humanae Vitae*, New York: Sheed and Ward, 1969; *idem*, 'Natural Law', in: *Themes in Fundamental Moral Theology*, Notre Dame: University of Notre Dame Press, 1977, pp. 27–69; *idem, Directions in*

Fundamental Moral Theology, Notre Dame: University of Notre Dame Press, 1985.
15. For this view on 'natural law', see J. Porter, *Nature as Reason: A Thomistic Theory of the Natural Law*, Grand Rapids/Cambridge: Eerdmans, 2005. Cf. also idem, *Natural and Divine Law: Reclaiming the Tradition for Christian Ethics*, Ottawa/Grand Rapids: Novalis/Eerdmans, 1999.
16. Thus M. Rhonheimer, *Natur als Grundlage der Moral: Die peronale Struktur des Naturgesetzes bei Thomas von Aquin – Eine Auseinandersetzung mit autonomer und teleologischer Ethik*, Innsbruck/Vienna: Tyrola, 1987, pp. 139–146 (Eng.trans. *Natural Law and Practical Reason: A Thomistic View of Moral Autonomy*, New York: Fordham University Press, 2000, pp. 138–45.
17. This is akin to the view of 'nature' as developed by Bruno Latour, see esp. his *Politics of Nature: How to Bring the Sciences into Democracy*, Cambridge: Harvard University Press, 2004. This view has also important consequences for a theological view on technology; cf. my 'Technology as Grace?', *Bulletin ET* 18 (2007) no. 1 (in print).
18. See for the religious and theological impact of the lives and the autobiographies of gay men on Catholic identity, D. McGinley, *Acts of Faith, Acts of Love: Gay Catholic Autobiographies as Sacred Texts*, New York & London: Continuum, 2004.
19. G. Moore, *The Body in Context: Sex and Catholicism*, London: SCM Press, 1992, p. 213.
20. In this way, I mean to refer to the theological approach of Edward Schillebeeckx, who started the project of developing a 'theology of culture' in the 1940s. See my *Edward Schillebeeckx: A Theologian in his History. Part I: A Catholic Theology of Culture 1914–1965*, London & New York: Continuum, 2003. *God the Future of Man* is the title of an important collection of articles by Schillebeeckx in the late 1960s (New York, London, & Sydney: Sheed & Ward, 1968).

On Queer Theory and Liberation Theology: The Irruption of the Sexual Subject in Theology

MARCELLA ALTHAUS-REID

My experiences with worlds that have seen me as Other have educated me on the negotiability of sustainable truths.

—George Mentore (2005: 16)

I. The burning of the flags

It was 15 August 2001, on the feast of the Assumption of the Virgin Mary. As the traditional Mass was ending in the cathedral of Santiago de Chile, a group of people were gathering at its doors. The voices from the last strains of the Mass were overlaid by the sounds of other different voices and songs. The people who had gathered at the door of the cathedral were activists from the *Movimiento de Integración y Liberación Homosexual* from Chile (MOVILH). They had come to protest against the Vatican's position in relation to homosexuality and more broadly about the fact that Chilean laws were closely bound to the teaching of the Church. Acts of protest such as this took place frequently in Latin America, but that day it was different: the demonstrators burnt the Vatican flag.[1] This event took place in Chile, a country in which the destinies of Church and State have been closely linked. It is significant that in Latin America there is no word to translate the English concept of 'secular'. It is commonly translated as *laico*, but that is itself a religious concept, viewing the contemporary world from the perspective of an ecclesiastical ideology. Thus, for example, the national civil law tends to parallel canonical law. Seen in this context, MOVILH's burning of the Vatican flag was not simply a disagreement among Christians, but an assertion of national sovereignty. This was made clear by the president of MOVILH in a statement to the press when he stated that the burning of the flag was a protest about the interference by the Vatican into the 'independence' (sovereignty) of national legislation on homosexuality. On this occasion the protestors were supporting not Chilean legislation but the kind of liberal laws on sexual rights to be found in the USA.

II. Vatican flag rules OK

The burning of the Vatican flag can be read as a complex narrative composed of several scandalous layers. It is a story of scandals upon scandals, as ideological borders are being constantly re-drafted, as people make different alliances to survive exclusion in a globalized world. Who could have envisaged that Chileans would one day publicly support the USA? That in itself has been scandalous for many. However, the fact is that sexuality, and specifically the theologies of sexuality, have historically played a crucial role in the re-marcation of the frontiers in Latin America. Take for instance the events of Buenos Aires in June 1945, when the Argentine parliament passed a law establishing the civil rights of those then classified as 'illegitimated children'. Statistics at the time show that in Buenos Aires alone nearly 200 out of 1000 children were classified under different categories such as *adulterinos* (born from adultery) or *incestuosos* (born from incestuous or not Church-approved relations). In the north of the country the numbers were even higher: 400 out of 1000 citizens were classified as religiously, politically, and socially illegitimate. To be so classified meant being denied the civil rights of the rest of the population. Illegitimate children were frequently failed by school systems and condemned to a life of exploitation at the margins of society.[2]

Yet, when the government decided to end the classification of children according to their accidental circumstances of birth, a Corpus Christi celebration was turned into a public demonstration by the Church: an Argentine flag in front of the cathedral of Buenos Aires was publicly replaced by a Vatican flag. The issues raised in the battle of the flags are many, but they can be summarized in one sentence. In Latin America, it is not which faith that counts, but which political alliance rules OK. Therefore Argentina 1945 and Chile 2001 are examples of the complex redrafting of legal theological borders between different claims of sovereignty – and both of them concerned sexual issues. As it happens sexuality is a public issue that affects multiple intersections of identity definitions amongst the Latin

American people. It is also the basis on which many are condemned to poverty and destitution (Solberg 1974:128).

Leaving aside the fact that we live in a world where flags are burnt everyday in different political settings such as G8 gatherings and foreign occupations, Chile is a country with a long history of struggle for human rights, forged in the decades of terror, when the country was under one of the most feared military regimes of the continent. This has left pedagogical historical lessons not only for people, who have learnt how to stand up for their rights, but also for the Church. I refer here in particular to the Chilean Church which, through the *Vicaría de la Solidaridad*[3] paid a high cost to defend those rights against a regime which set up concentration camps and curtailed even the most basic civil rights.

III. Sexuality and the Option for the Poor

As if the scandal of the burning of the Vatican flag and the apparent gay alliance with USA legal rights were not enough, there was a further twist to the story of these events, which brings to light the deep-seated complexity of queer theology and sexuality. The further development was that the president of *TravesChile*, one of the largest organizations of transvestites in the country, wrote and signed an open letter to the Church distancing the transvestite Chilean community from the events. 'We are deeply disturbed', the letter reads, 'and we ask the Church for forgiveness, as we want to make clear that MOVILH and its president ... do not represent the whole of the homosexual communities in Chile. We (transvestites) are deeply devoted to the Virgin Mary.'[4] This episode, constructed around so many layers of oppression, is still remembered as the 'Gay betrayal' by the Chilean transvestites of the homosexual movement in Latin America. However, it may not have been a betrayal at all: it is its complexity that allows us to explore crucial issues in our reflections on theology, queer theory, and sexuality.

The Latin American Church has what might be called a long liberationist history running in its veins. Hunger and the devastating effects of social deprivation are everyday facts of life that no Church, irrespective of its theological position, can afford to ignore. Orthodox or liberal, Christian people need to eat. In other words, the marginalized are not part of an *Otherness* discourse but are the same people who fill the pews in our Churches every Sunday. In a continent where even the most otherworldly of the Churches arriving from the USA will probably end sooner or later organizing some soup kitchen, the feeding of the poor has a sacramental status. Yet homosexuals, in spite of their marginalization and even the impunity with which crimes are at times committed against them, have never been the concern of any Church, conservative or liberationist, till now. Except for one group, the transvestites. Let us consider briefly why.

There may be several complex reasons for the fact that transvestites have been, in some cases, included into the ample spectrum of the Church's option for the margins. For a start, transvestites in Latin America constitute one of the poorest and most vulnerable groups of marginalized people. There may be other reasons, such as how, in an extremely patriarchal continent where women's gender construction is severely sanctioned and stereotyped, cross-dressers with a high feminine performativity could be perceived as less threatening than gays. In this, the media has a lot to answer for. Some of the patronizing elements in transvestite identities in Latin America are perhaps coincident with female gender construction. Transvestites are portrayed in the media as archetypes of femininity and coquetry, not necessarily as intellectuals but as people with strong emotional lives. How many times I have heard the common expression that transvestites need a lot of affection in their lives! The dualism rationality-emotion has been re-inscribed in the transvestite body.

Is it that sense of performed feminine vulnerability, even quasi-domesticity, which the media is so keen to use to portray transvestites, that makes them appear as a fragile but also dependent group? Is it that that attracts the compassion of the Church? It may be so: or perhaps that there are reasons to be compassionate with transvestites as a group. They are amongst the poorest of the poor and the most legally unprotected. In fact, prostitution seems to be the only job option available, even when transvestites themselves have long fought for the possibility to find other employment.

IV. With threads and needles we mend blouses

During the time of the events leading to the burning of the Vatican flag the Chilean Church had been supporting educational projects for transvestites such as classes in sewing, cooking, and hairdressing. A short course entitled *Con Hilos y Agujas Zurcimos Cierres y Blusas* ('With threads and needles we mend zips and blouses') was very successful. There was also a church initiative to create soup kitchens for them. *TravesChile* has a photograph on its web page showing a priest blessing a meal in one of these soup kitchens, while the transvestites are sitting around the table in an attitude of prayer. It is not an issue of sexuality, but of poverty and need.

That support from the Church in terms of social projects but also of affection and care may have been the real reason why they repudiated the burning of the Vatican flag. Transvestites sensed that the Church was giving them love in action in a society and in religious structures that had long abandoned them.

There are two important matters on which to reflect here though. First, to recognize that in Chile the Church made an option not for transvestites, but for poor transvestites. Second, that there is no homogeneity either in issues of identity or in common experiences of objectives around issues of oppression. That became clear in the fact that transvestites and gays have, as groups, different interests and a different history of oppression. There may be different ideological alliances and confrontations, for instance according to issues of class and race. Also patriarchalism as an ideology may have impacted more on gays than on lesbians and transvestites.

In these reflections we are already using a queer conceptualization of sexuality, although we have not been yet specific. In queer theory there is no assumption of homogeneous sexual identities amongst people, as there is no homogeneity amongst heterosexual people themselves. Moreover, for queer theory sexual identities are not stable and necessarily coincident with political of religious foundations. That is true also of the instability of heterosexuality although it has been an approved sexual ideology.

Queer theory becomes important as we consider theological issues of sexuality because, hermeneutically, theology needs to confront the irruption of the sexual subject in history, in the same way that liberationists confronted the irruption of the Church of the poor or the 'underdogs of history' (Gutiérrez 1988:88). The construction of the unitary subject, both in sexual or in colonial studies, operates according to principles of power and subjection, but in times of postcolonial awareness, theology should know better.

V. Queer and liberationists

If the irruption of the sexual subject *per se* (outside for instance, the category of 'the poor') is polemical, let us remember that any attempt by the Church to develop a theology with a new theological subject has always been confrontational and polemical. The last few decades have provided many examples of this. There have been the poor as theological subject, followed by women at the centre of feminist theology, followed also by contextual Black and Asian theologies, which expressed the struggle to give autonomy to the Other in theology.

What happens is that the irruption of the Other complicates everybody's life: the life of theology, theologians, and the Church. Why? Because to take on board Otherness means much more than to include the different into a familiar discourse, as in indigenization, which is a form of co-optation. To take on board Otherness implies taking on also the hermeneutical and ecclesiastical challenges presented by a previously silenced subject. This subject definition is unrepresented and unrepresentable by the system that has produced a symbolic exclusion in the first place. That is to say, it is not only a thematic change that confronts us, but a radical criticism of existing theological methodologies, which are abortive, as they cut the living potentialities of the Other from our midst.

The Other, by reason of gender, race, class, or sexuality not only brings a criticism to theology but also incarnates a living criticism, as the biblical blood of the just that cries out to God for crimes committed against the different in any theological orthodoxy. The historically insignificant (as Gutiérrez puts it), that is, those not worthy of signifying socially, politically, or theologically, constitute the revelatory horizon of the Church. And revelation is an epistemological issue.

VI. On the sexual subject of theology

The sexual subject has always been theologically insignificant. For that reason sexual theology has never existed as such: we do not even have a proper theology of relationships such as marriage. We do have liturgical developments and laws, but historically we have missed the opportunity to learn from people's actual sexual experiences. For this reason the Church lacks serious reflection in this area. As gender studies confronted theology with the ideological construction of female (and male) roles in society, the Church has only responded by barricading itself against the possibility of taking seriously the real sexual subjects of history.

The control of heterosexual behaviour and gender assignment have been developed over a long time in the Church. But this is not the end of the matter. Gay and later on lesbian theologies developed from changes of sexual paradigms. New challenges to theology have arisen from the medicalization of sexuality. There is a notable distance between mediaeval biology and an understanding of sexuality within processes of political and religious power. As gay and lesbian theologies challenged issues of sexuality but also social and political issues, the sexual epistemological foundations of Christianity needed to be re-thought from the perspective of a new sexual theological subject.

Yet, the journey has not finished there: it continues with what we call queer theory. Queer theory is constructionist, but so is gender theory. Gender behaviour is not understood as part of the immutable laws of God. However, queer theory goes further, analyzing not just the construction of gender, but of sexualities as ideological productions. Therefore, let us consider now the 'queer thing' in more detail.

VII. On queer theory

"Hey, queer!" No response. No confession.
—Donald Hall (2003: 18)

In common with liberation theologies, queer theory comes from an appropriation of terms of derision and rejection. The term 'queer', originally a term of abuse, has been appropriated in a positive sense in order to lay the stress on elements of unconventionality, nonconformity, and disruption. However, although we may have become accustomed to it, the same can be said about the phrase 'Church of the poor' or 'popular theology'. It is easy to forget today, after decades of a positive discourse concerning the preferential option of the poor by God in history, that the poor were never considered a worthy theological subject in their own right. Also, popular culture was never considered a worthy theological partner. Some years ago, when I first settled in Britain, I was questioned by my editors on my use of the term 'popular theology' which they assumed meant theology that was not academic, perhaps ironic.

As with liberationists, queer theory did not originate in academic circles but as the result of activism from the margins. It comes from the Chicana women's movement in the USA, who disagreed with the cultural, racial, and class implications of the definition (and normativity) imposed on their lesbian identities by privileged discourse within the USA. Coincidentally, there was a time when indigenous people felt unrepresented when confronted by the homogeneous identity of the poor in the Latin American discourse of liberation. There were also women, indigenous and urban, who broke with the idealism of blanket definitions of poverty. That complicated the life of liberationists who wanted a unified subject for many reasons, including strategic.

The problem is that theology is not used to having an unstable subject: instead, it behaves as a constitutional, judicial system where exceptions are not viable, unless they become recognized exceptions. Queer theory also broke with the written laws of sexual identities in different ways. First, it brought to the light different sexual subjects such as bisexuals and transvestites. Second, it refused to confer any homogenous identities on different sexual options. Third, it argued that sexuality, like gender, is taught and rehearsed. That is precisely the pedagogical aspect of gender. To teach a woman how to dress, how to perform certain tasks, or even how to walk or how to speak with a particular tone of voice, is to teach a woman to become a woman. This is what Butler calls gender performativity in a nutshell: 'the tacit collective agreement to perform, produce, and sustain discrete and polar genders as cultural fictions'. And she adds that those who defy 'the credibility of those productions' are punished (Butler 1990:140). Gender requires belief: no wonder gender disbelief underlies many sins.

But let us think more precisely about queer theory. The development of this research owes much to the original work of Michel Foucault, Eve Kosofsky Sedgwick, and Judith Butler. Michael Warner defines queer in the following way: '[Queer] represents... a resistance to regimes of the normal' (Warner 1993: xxvi). 'Normality' is here an ideological construction the consequences of which affect not only economic and cultural productions but also the socio-religious production of people's sense of identity. The conceptualization of sexual identity is a relatively recent one. It arose from the medical discourses of the late nineteenth century, but biological sexual identity representations in theology date from Aristotle via Augustine, who found incest and rape more agreeable than masturbation and homosexuality (Hampson 2002:189). Theologians have been using not only biological determinism in their conceptualization of sexuality but unscientific, medieval thinking that they would not entertain for a moment in other spheres such as economics or communications.

Queer theory then explores the question of identity, and we can see how this becomes a challenge for the Church in the construction of the theological subject. In queer theory, as in the case of the transvestites from Chile in opposition to the gay movement (at least, on that occasion), the key is diversity. The same is true of the understanding of diversity that the indigenous nations of Latin America have been demanding for centuries, since the so-called discovery. 'Discovery' could have been a good and positive thing, for it could have meant the encounter with the Other, without the need to destroy the Other and erase cultural, religious, and political differences. A respect for diversity is what Black and Asian theologies ask. Their right to define their own identities is important for them: it is crucial theologically speaking, since identity formation processes are not neutral.

Therefore queer theory can be considered as an umbrella term, covering the study of processes of sexual identity formation in relation to power. That includes the regimes of normality dictated by racial and class ideologies.

VIII. Queer theology

There is a 'one' who is prior to gender.
—Butler (1993:21)

Queer theology (or theologies, to be more precise) is the complex result of a theological reflection that considers what the different constructions of sexuality and gender have to say of our understanding of God, love, and community. Queer theory was influenced by the post-structuralist movement, which argued against the notion of a stable subject and confronted the ideological formation of sexual identities. From its reflections, two main elements of theological inquiry need to be considered. First, a suspicion concerning the assumption that heterosexuality is a universal and stable sexual identity and as such part of a natural (sacralized) order. Second, the realization of the fact that hegemonic constructions of sexual identity have historically contributed to the consolidation of oppressive structures of power relationships in the Christian Church and in theology.

If this sounds like a post-modern trend, let us remember that issues of power and identity in theology are older than the post-modern movement. In fact, theology has never been a stranger to disputes on ideological matters of identity: the twentieth century saw the emergence of many contextual theologies. Black American, African, Feminist, Indigenous, and Post-colonial theologies, amongst others, are precisely the result of a queering of the universalistic assumptions of the identity of the theological subject as produced by the colonial tendencies of North Atlantic theology. Feminist theology was the first to identify the ideologies of gender which supported a patriarchal discourse of power in classical theology, where categories of 'normal' or 'natural' were sacralized as the divine will. By not taking into account the differences amongst theological subjects, theology ignored the historical, religious experience and thought not of minorities but, on the contrary, majorities. Multitudes of women, black people, indigenous communities, or gays became subjected to the theological hierarchical structures of religious and social discrimination, control and oppression.

However important gender categories have been, queer theologies see them as less crucial to processes of identity formation in theology than discourses on sexuality. As early as the mid-1970s gay and lesbian theologies identified heterosexuality as a pervasive and formative ideology that contributed not just to the creation of a structure of inequality and violence but to the ignoring of the religious experience of non-heterosexuals. As John D'Emilio demonstrated, heterosexuality and homosexuality were categories related to nineteenth-century emergent industrial capitalism (D'Emilio 1977:170). Therefore, sexual identities are not natural but construed identities, closely related to socio-political and cultural understandings and lacking the internal coherence and historical stability attributed to them. Gay and lesbian identities were then viewed as the result of the struggle for justice and peace of non-heterosexual sexual groups. Sexual identities are not to be defined biologically but politically. In that sense and in their disputation of the authority of heterosexuality as the only valid epistemological foundation of Church and society, sexual theologies such as lesbian and gay and queer theologies have common interests, although differences remain. The main difference lies in the understanding that if both homosexuality and heterosexuality are construed identities, there are other sexualities that do not necessarily fit either of these categories. Moreover, if homosexuality is a category invented by and grounded on heterosexual understandings, it may carry within itself characteristics of heterosexual thinking. In other words, queer theory not only challenges heterosexuality as an ideology but considers that non-heterosexual identities may have been developed around the axis of internal coherence by which heterosexuality organizes itself. For instance, there is a controversy in gay circles over gay marriage. Should marriage, an affective but also economic institution developed within patriarchal heterosexuality, be adopted, or modified?

Theologically speaking, there are deep challenges that come from questioning the epistemological status of heterosexuality. Even the term 'non-heterosexual' has been developed within a colonial conceptual dependency and perpetuates the idea of the ideological primacy of heterosexuality. Queer theology, then, by reclaiming sexual identities outside the conceptual binary opposition between heterosexuality and homosexuality, brings other theological subjects and sexual epistemologies into consideration, for instance, bisexualism, transgenderism, and transsexualism. Queer theology also provides a critical reflection on the social construction of heterosexuality and how heterosexual thinking affects also heterosexual people themselves.

Queer theories are complex. One of the most important queer scholars, Judith Butler, has developed a sophisticated theory of the role of gender in heterosexual formations based on the figure of the Drag Queen as a pedagogical resource by which gender has been impersonated or theatralized (as already observed). Drags are about imitation and the imitation of a specific gender that, in reality, does not exist. It depends precisely on their superficial production, as if being a woman depended on a way to dress, to adorn the hair, to sit with legs crossed. That imitation of genders she calls 'performativity', which interpellates the spectator in a pedagogical way. We should recall that 'interpellation' is the term that Althusser uses to explain how ideologies co-opt people instead of generating resistance. Similarly, Freire has called internalization of oppression the way that the oppressed majorities of Latin Americans tended to obey their masters without questioning.

Genders are then imitations without originals, yet it is through them that a woman learns to be a woman and a man, a man. In order to sustain its claim of naturalness, heterosexuality also needs to repeat permanently its own gender acts. Yet, heterosexuality's own repetitive strategies may prove the point that genders are only pedagogical devices of which one of the main functions is to teach the prevalent sexual identity. For Butler, a strategy for change would be to disrupt the performance of the regime of the normal as inscribed in gender repetitions.

IX. Final reflections: on risk-taking theologies.

[The risk is] to aspire not to go towards the deepest (knowledge) but instead, to the most innocent one.
—Yuderkys Espinosa-Miñoso (2004:143; my translation)

This brings us to the last point in our reflections. We have considered the relevance and challenges of a theology open to new historical subjects. However, we should go on to ask, in the light of queer theory, how the construction of compulsory heterosexuality has influenced and compromised our understanding of God and the Church. Also, following a liberationist preoccupation with praxis, how can we effectively help the communities of poor transvestites to have agency in respect of their own identity (and Christian identity) during the process? My response is that these are important issues for a queer theology of compassion and action, which will involve also a dialogical process of mutual learning and sharing. Perhaps the Church has much to learn from the presence of God amongst the poor, black women, and transvestites too.

Queer sexuality understands the imprecision of human identities. That in itself is a powerful element of resistance, not just to authoritative sexual discourse, but to the ideological domestication of God. Reading the history of the Church through these lenses means that hidden, disruptive sexual elements in Church history and traditions are unveiled. Queer theologians have also been active in producing strategies for reading the scriptures in order to claim a subject different from that assumed for the texts[5]. This uncovers elements of subversion and challenge to the regimes of the 'normal' in the interpretation of the word of God. Queer theory also has implications for Christian ethics and practical theology, in questioning for instance the sexual economies of the Christian family and marriage, the inclusion/exclusion of the body in Christian liturgy, and the regulation of spirituality. Queer theologies have contributed to reflections on the sacraments, christology, and dogmatics. Yet queer theologies are plural theologies. There are contextual emphases and different approaches that depend on the historical circumstances and needs of specific communities.

As a Latin American theologian I have developed a project of queering liberation theology, relating queer theory and Marxist thought. Other colleagues, such as Tom Hanks and Nancy Cardoso Pereira,[6] also have been producing a sophisticated theological reflection, mixing class analysis with queer suspicion.

Queer theology is a critical theology that addresses that element which sustains all the discourses and public battles of the Church, namely sexuality. It should not be a theology of 'sexual inclusivity' but of difference. It is a call to produce a queer, Christ-centred theology of reflection and action, a call to a socially committed and transformative discipleship in the midst of those powerful ideological statements expressed through race, gender, sexuality, and class, which have pervaded previous Christian theologies. But queer theologies are not without a need for self reflection and criticism.

Some theologians are unhappy with the erasure of sexual identities produced by queer theory, especially if it fails to take into account the political struggles of gays and lesbians to establish their identities. Also, some queer theologians, in the course of their work may become *déraciné/es*, uprooted from the lives of communities, or unconsciously dominated by class and racial assumptions of privilege in their discourse.

To conclude, queer theologies by their nature resist simple definitions. They are contextual theologies with an option for those at the margin of heterosexual ideologies. As such, they are deconstructivist theologies, which challenge the sex-gender binary system of Christian theology while aiming to transform all structures of sin in society. As the original liberationists used to claim, the goal at the end is to liberate God Godself from the ideological structures of oppression that Christianity has historically constructed around the understanding of the sacred, the reading of the scriptures and the vision of how to be a Church. Liberation theologians in the twentieth century took many risks: they paid a high price, some with their lives, with their commitment to the gospel amongst the excluded. In this new century the risks have not diminished as poverty, destitution, and the impunity of a globalized system of injustice become more difficult to contest. In all this, the task of unveiling sexual ideologies in theology is no small thing. It is a major contribution to the historical liberation of the power of God's love and the message of the gospel at a time when the poor have started to become theological subjects. The struggle to liberate the love of God from our own transient, ideological constructions of sexual, gender, racial, religious, or cultural power must continue amongst the faithful.

Bibliography

Althaus-Reid, M. (2000). *Indecent Theology*. London: Routledge.
——(ed.) (2005). *Liberation Theology and Sexuality*. London: Ashgate.
Butler, J. (1990). *Gender Troubles. Feminism and the Subversion of Identity*. London: Routledge.
——(1993). 'Critically Queer'. *GLQ: A Journal of Lesbian and Gay Studies* 1 (1): 21.
Goss, R. (1993). *Jesus Acted Up. A Gay and Lesbian Manifesto*. Scranton: Harper Collins.
D'Emilio, J. (1997). 'Capitalism and Gay Identity,' in M. Lancaster and M. Di Leonardo (eds), *The Gender/Sexuality Reader*. London: Routledge.
Gutiérrez, G. (1988). *A Liberation Theology*. Maryknoll, NY: Orbis.
Hall, D. E. (2003). *Queer Theories*. Hampshire: Palgrave.

Mentore, G. (2005). *Of Passionate Curves and Desirable Cadences. Themes on Waiwai Social Being*. Lincoln: University of Nebraska Press.
Espinosa-Miñones, Y. (2004). 'A una década de la performatividad: de percepciones erróneas y malos entendidos', in J. Fernández, M. D'Uva and P. Viturro (eds) *Cuerpos Ineludibles*. Buenos Aires: Ají de Pollo.
Warner, M. (1993) 'Introduction,' in M Warner (ed.) *Fear of a Queer Planet: Queer Politics and Social Theory*. Minneapolis: Univ. of Minnesota Press, vii-xxxi.

Notes

1. For more details see the article 'Homosexuales quemaron bandera del Vaticano en frontis de Catedral Chilena', in *Opus Gay, Primer Periódico Gay de Chile*. Available online at http://www.opusgay.cl/1315/article-36183.html
2. Cf the article from Carl Solberg, 'Farm Workers and the Myth of Export-Led Development in Argentina' in *The Americas*, Vol. 31, No 2 (Oct 1974), 121–38. The author's main thesis is that the so-called illegitimate children, through their lack of access to educational systems and marginalization, contributed to the cheap labour force of Argentina till the 1950s. The 1945 law may have had as its objective to educate and integrate the Argentine work force in a new industrialized era.
3. The *Vicaría de la Solidaridad* (Vicariate of Solidarity) was created in Chile by Pope Paul VI by petition of Archbishop Raúl Silva Henríquez. From 1976 to 1992 it functioned as an organism of the Church for the defence of Human Rights. Today, it continues as an archival resource of more than 80,000 testimonies and procedures taken by the Church to help families during the Chilean dictatorial regime.
4. Cf. 'Carla Antonelli Diario Digital de Información Transexual', Agosto 2003. Available on line at http://www.carlaantonelli.com/agosto%20%202003%20noticias%20transexuales.html, p14.
5. See for instance Tom Hanks's article 'Good News for Sexual Workers' in Robert Goss and Mona West (eds) *Take Back the Word. A Queer Reading of the Bible*. Cleveland: The Pilgrim Place, 2000.
6. For a reading of Latin American liberation theologians working on queer theology, see my edited book *Liberation Theology and Sexuality*, London: Ashgate, 2005.

Encountering Beasts: Lesbian Biblical Hermeneutics on the Road

DERYN GUEST

This journal's title provided the inspiration for what I might write in this paper: *concilio*, bringing together, *reconcilio*, the work of reconciliation, and the act of bringing thoughts to be evaluated at the council, the *concilium*. Accordingly, rather than write further about lesbian biblical hermeneutics or provide additional examples of its application,[1] I shall write about the motivations that produced the lesbian biblical hermeneutics project and how it could be understood in terms of reconciliation. When initiating that project I was motivated academically by the thought of expanding the feminist agenda in biblical studies – defining in depth some principles and strategies for lesbian biblical interpretation. But personally there was the desire to bring to a wider audience the lesbian interpretations of biblical texts already in existence. I hoped to show how the Bible can similarly be a place of lesbian playfulness and joy, for I understood only too well how Jews and Christians who identify as lesbians have to make an effort to integrate these identities, or deal with the renunciation of one over the other. The first section of this paper thus discusses how the first act of reconciliation could be seen in terms of the contribution lesbian biblical hermeneutics might make for those who identify as lesbian and who struggle to square this with their allegiances to scriptures that are often deployed to condemn their choices.

However there is a second audience in view: those who would deploy the Bible to disseminate anti-lesbian rhetoric. At the foundation of religious positional statements on homosexuality is usually a small clutch of texts on which an entire debate hinges: Gen. 19; Lev. 18.22; 20.13; Rom. 1.18–32; 1 Cor. 6.9 and 1 Tim 1.9–10, together with selected verses from Genesis 1 – 3. Left in the hands of interpreters who erroneously assume that these texts bear a relation to twenty-first century consenting lesbian relationships, they are made to speak – across the centuries and geographical divides – of God's unequivocal condemnation. Fearful and righteously indignant about secular legislation that appears to be undermining God's intentions for (heterosexual) humanity, religious authority figures present themselves as the guardians of scriptural truth, as the embattled and beleaguered defenders of God's revealed intentions for humankind.

In this context, a voice for lesbian biblical interpretation is vital, not only for resisting those texts of terror and their use in the contemporary world, but also in reclaiming scriptural stories in ways that demonstrate how the Bible is not a one-directional piece of ammunition. Lesbian biblical interpretation is an act of political activism; it puts forward its own distinctive contribution so that committees and councils working out religious positional statements are confronted with alternative visions. Ultimately one hopes that the debate will progress so that not just token toleration, but full welcome acceptance for *practising*, happy lesbian Christians and Jews can be won. The potential knock-on effects would be substantial: an end to the religious opposition to progressive legislation which now sanctions the rights of lesbians to form civil partnerships/marry, adopt children, and live their lives protected from discrimination. An end to the prevention of practising lesbians playing a full role in religious life as youth workers, priests, rabbis. And there would be far more significant benefit for lesbians in non-western countries where oppression on the basis of religious discourse is more overt and sustained. In short, there was/is a hope of some reconciliation with religious wings that would use the Bible to withstand such moves and to exclude lesbians from civil and religious life.

These two things – reconciliation in terms of healing oneself from internalized homonegativity and reconciliation in terms of engaging with those who would use the Bible to condemn – do not happen in isolation but are interlocked, and it is difficult for one to proceed without the other. Moreover, while the reconciliation envisaged for the former appears to be able to proceed relatively smoothly, reconciliation in terms of the latter venture has been much more of a bumpy road, littered with beasts and spectres of paedophiles. This paper will address the issues that have arisen when taking lesbian biblical hermeneutics 'on the road' and attempt to unpack some of the resistance to reconciliation that I have met.

I. Reconciling oneself to oneself

Lesbians brought up in religious contexts are prone to receiving negative messages about their gender and sexual choices. The effects of this should not be understated: they can be long-term and toxic. Internalized homophobia from years of religious upbringing has been identified as a real problem by therapists who also recognize that lesbian-friendly biblical interpretation can offer a beneficial, therapeutic aid to recovery.[2] It can help to restore oneself to oneself not only by finding our lives and loves resonating with scriptural events and characters, or by enjoying the delightful queer readings of unexpected texts, but by being able to express anger and resentment through lesbian readings of texts.[3]

Of course, post-structuralists unsettle the concept that there is a 'oneself' to find. One can believe that one has 'arrived' at a core sense of a lesbian identity only to find that the journey is on-going or contradictory.[4] There can, for example, be shifts from a lesbian to a trans- or bisexual self-understanding, or the adoption of queer rather than a lesbian positioning. There can be contradiction between a public 'out and proud' performance and the moments of inner doubt and turmoil. Reconciliation with oneself thus is ongoing; a journeying with oneself. Aspects of lesbian biblical hermeneutics may accordingly find greater resonance at certain life moments only.

This connects with my growing conviction that there will always be a place for the early lesbian and gay theologies from which queer theologies sometimes distance themselves. Consider the 'stage' theories prominent in sociological and psychological literature.[5] So long as it is recognized that there is not a linear progression but a spiralling journey that is fraught with digressions, and also that there is no 'one size fits all' theory, the general notion that there are recognizable passages to be encountered as one moves from default heteronormative expectations to lesbian affirmation seems feasible. Lesbian theology and/or biblical hermeneutics is likely to have greater resonance at various points of this journey. Thus, when Paula Rust talks about the need to 'grieve the loss of heterosexual identity and social relationships as well as the previously taken-for-granted sense of belonging to mainstream society and culture' one can imagine how that sense of grief is exacerbated significantly when loss of one's religious home is taken into account, as some literature testifies.[6] What one needs at these times, and in contexts where being out or queer simply isn't a safe option, may be less a bold and celebratory queer theology and more the work of an early pioneer like John J. McNeill, whose psychotherapy-informed work still fruitfully addresses the issues faced when first emerging in religious contexts that are far from hospitable. Similarly, I believe that lesbian biblical interpretation can provide a conciliatory function that helps lesbian-identified people come to terms with scriptures and interpret them from their own perspectives, at certain stages of their life-journey. The lesbian biblical hermeneutics project, accordingly, is not a static thing but needs always to be in flux and in possession of a whole toolbox of diverse strategies that can be drawn upon.

However, poststructural thinking also reminds us that the notion of the self is actually an ongoing work that happens in the process of social interaction with others. The art of reconciling oneself with oneself is thus also about the work of reconciliation with surrounding discourses, beliefs, and values. This has contributed to a shift in thinking about the language of 'internalized homophobia' (which puts the focus on lesbians as objects, and repathologizes them)[7] to the alternative term, 'homonegating processes', which puts the focus where it should be – on the interlocking social, political, religious, familial discourses that construct what Russell and Bohan call an 'attitudinal fog' which is 'laced with homonegativity' and renders us all participants in the creation and performance of homophobia. This is as true of those who identify as LGBT as it is of those who do not. Accordingly, what has been termed 'internalized homophobia' is better understood as the unavoidable reiteration of pervasive and largely unreflective cultural beliefs. LGBT people simply express and enact the attitudes that they have absorbed by virtue of their participation in the culture.[8]

Their conclusion is that when it comes to homonegativity, 'none of us is simply the villain or the victim; and that it is the fog, not its ventriloquators, that needs to be addressed'.[9] The reference to ventriloquation is interesting. It is a term used by Bakhtin to describe the way in which we all act as dummies, sitting on the lap of our collective certainties, instruments of the expression of those certainties. We all absorb the messages, and without consciously intending to propagate stereotypes, we regularly ventriloquate cultural assumptions in our own language and actions, simply reiterating or rehearsing what we have so thoroughly absorbed, what we are certain is true. In the process, we contribute to the further creation and dissemination of the same beliefs.[10]

Russell and Bohan go on to point out that since ventriloquation is communal, staying within the parameters of the same socio-linguistic community means that one will find 'repeated confirmation for the beliefs we utter, and these confirmations reproduce the phenomena we bespeak'.[11] Translating this into the context of our discussion, it helps explain why the 'battle for the Bible' continues to be fought *ad nauseam*. Ventriloquism reinforces certainty about one's constructed beliefs and values and speaks them into existence. For LGBT people who are directly affected by the discourse of anti-gay religious pronouncements, the impact is substantial, whereas for those in the sexual majority, the message has far less impact insofar as the messages are affirming of heteronormativity. However, as Russell and Bohan recognize, placing homonegativity firmly in the social domain means that it is not only constructed but also *subject to alteration* by collective discourse: 'The notion that all of us are equally subject to homophobic and heterosexist narratives renders the responsibility and opportunity for their amelioration a collective task'.[12]

In the present climate of religious homonegativity, such reconciliatory work is always going to be very difficult. There is a dissonant clash of beliefs that will not easily be resolved unless we all look up from the narrow confines of the debate and are prepared to admit and take responsibility for our part in ventriloquation. I am not sanguine about the chances of this happening in the near future given the experiences that are recounted below.

II. Reconciling those who engage in condemning discourse with pro-lesbian biblical interpretation

Reconciliation has to be at least two-sided. As I take lesbian biblical hermeneutics into various contexts where I have been invited/employed to speak, discomfort is often visible, and often this manifests itself in two typical responses. First, an accusation: lesbian interpretation is a matter of wishful thinking/special pleading. Second, a question: would I be equally happy listening to readings of scripture that derive from groups engaging in bestiality and/or paedophilia? I was not surprised by the accusation since queer theorists regularly face such claims, but I was somewhat taken aback by the connection with bestiality, until I found from discussions with colleagues that they had been similarly questioned.[13] It is worth taking the time to unpack what might be going on with these complaints, for they clearly stand as obstacles to any conciliatory progress.

When queer practitioners make robust claims like this: 'Our reading of texts is an act of perversion. It takes the authoritative version of a reading, perverts or deconstructs it, and offers a counter-reading or an alternative version,'¹⁴, it seems only to confirm an audience's worst suspicions. But the significant part of this quotation is what comes next: it is an alternative version *'that does not pretend to finality or authority. It leaves our readings tentative, open to further interrogation and critical dispute, and to new emergent meanings'*.¹⁵ It seems that this is actually the basis of the discomfort: the possibility that the Bible does not have a 'fixed' interpretation that can be appealed to in safety, with certitude, which confirms for all time and in all places God's hatred of homosexuality. When lesbian biblical readings are criticized for being partisan one almost hears the sigh of relief: it's just lesbians trying to make the Bible say what it doesn't say, i.e.: I don't have to listen to this twaddle. There is scant recognition that *all* biblical interpretation is interested, that there is no fixed and authoritative word – just dominant community readings to which members of that community adhere. What is at stake here is who 'owns' the 'correct' (i.e. dominant) interpretation of the Bible. And what is actively suppressed is the fact that *all acts of interpretation are interested*. In the academic world, despite the continued dominance of the historical-critical approach, the hermeneutical circle is a widely-acknowledged phenomenon, and the rise of feminist, Black, postcolonial, and autobiographical approaches bear witness to this. But this does not yet seem to have pervaded fully the lay world, where commitment to the 'final word' of scripture combines with the assumption that one's interpretation of those scriptures is unclouded by bias or contextual influences. This produces a hard, fixed position, which cannot allow that it is actually the result of conscious or unconscious interpretative choices.¹⁶ It is a way of cutting the ground from beneath the speaker's feet. When one can confidently appeal to the clobber texts noted above and a huge weight of heterosexist interpretative tradition, it is relatively easy to wave away dismissively any attempts to re-evaluate such texts (since the assumption of partisanship can be readily invoked), and to squint incredulously at gay-friendly interpretations of other stories. For example, upon hearing a positive lesbian reclamation of stories such as Ruth and Naomi there is an immediate appeal to Ruth's marriage to Boaz. Any reading that privileges her loving relationship with Naomi is simply the result of special pleading.

Such reactions seem to be manifestations of the desire to displace one's own discomfort by forcing it upon the invited speaker, willing them to admit defeat and step down from such 'wild speculation'. It is far easier to attack the other, albeit with polite courtesy, than to be self-critical of the interested nature of one's own privileged and long-standing interpretations. The only interpreter with bias has to be the lesbian interpreter. But this misses the point, for as Alpert makes clear, lesbian readings are not trying to prove that the story actually happened this way, but to make room for change within tradition while providing historical antecedent for the change. Making room for lesbian interpretation of the Book of Ruth is a way of welcoming lesbians into the contemporary Jewish community.[17]

Moreover, when it comes to reading Micah 6.8 or the Psalms, attempts to dismiss the interpretation become arguably more difficult. Kamionkowski recognizes that the fact that the Psalms can be queered 'does not mean that they are necessarily translesbigay-friendly' but her readings nonetheless demonstrate that 'No single group can claim exclusive access to this rich body of religious poetry', and her work boldly shakes up assumptions about how the Psalter can be read. Alpert's reading of Micah 6.8 does not appeal to the close friendship of biblical female characters, but to biblical injunctions to walk in honesty and dignity before God.[18]

Reading the prophets or the Psalms through a lesbian lens is unexpected and seemingly more unnerving. Maybe this accounts for the responses that place my life-choices on a continuum with bestiality and paedophilia. This seems to be a knee-jerk reaction; a self-defence mechanism that halts this (more persuasive?) strand of lesbian interpretation in its tracks before it can 'contaminate'. It is a means not only of rejecting but also *debasing* and denouncing what is being heard. The 'logic' it relies upon is a shared view that bestial or paedophilia interests would never have a justifiable place at the table of biblical interpretation. Enjoining those listening to agree that no one would want to entertain readings from communities who engage in bestiality or paedophilia is a way of trying to gain widespread support and then using this as a platform to criticize lesbian readings (which are equally 'detestable').

The anxiety/fear is understandable. Lesbian biblical hermeneutics strike at the heart of heteronormativity and the role the Bible has played in reinforcing it, opening the eyes to the fact that conventional readings of scripture have not only been androcentric, Eurocentric, often anti-Semitic, imperialistic, but also heterosexist. Challenging this is tantamount to challenging the huge default assumption that a heterosexist society is the God-willed, superior, and ordained order for humankind.

If there were an entirely satisfying repost to this, we probably would not need to have this discussion and the 'battle for the Bible' might be well on its way to resolution. But so long as flinging wide the doors to lesbians, gays, transgenderists, bisexuals, drag kings and queens, or fetishists is suspected as the beginning of a feared slippery slope to a radical inclusion of 'unrepentant sinners', progress will always be difficult.

Gayle Rubin's work has relevance here. The concept of a slippery slope is clearly pictured in her notion of sex hierarchy. Her first figure has a small 'charmed circle' which include relations that are heterosexual, married, monogamous, procreative, non-commercial, in pairs, in a relationship, same generation, in private, no pornography, bodies only, and vanilla: this is the 'Good, Normal, Natural, Blessed Sexuality'. This circle is embraced by an outer circle ('Bad, Abnormal, Unnatural, Damned Sexuality') and refers to sex that 'may be homosexual, unmarried, promiscuous, non-procreative, or commercial. It may be masturbatory or take part at orgies, may be casual, may cross generational lines, and may take place in "public". . . It may involve the use of pornography, fetish objects, sex toys, or unusual roles.'[19] As she comments, the arguments are 'conducted over "where to draw the line," and to determine what other activities, if any, may be permitted to cross over into acceptability'.[20] Her second figure is of brick walls, and there is a close match between this diagram and my encounters with the bestiality issue. There is, says Rubin, a 'domino theory of sexual peril' and the walls 'stand between sexual order and chaos. It expresses the fear that if anything is permitted to cross this erotic DMZ, the barrier against scary sex will crumble and something unspeakable will skittle across'.[21] Thus, while coupled, monogamous homosexuality may be able to straddle the wall, 'promiscuous homosexuality, sadomasochism, fetishism, transsexuality, and cross-generational encounters are still viewed as unmodulated horrors incapable of involving affection, love, free choice, kindness or transcendence'.[22]

Fears, anxieties, ignorance, and unwillingness to cherish difference characterize this hierarchy. However, Rubin places the focus on mutual consent, consideration, kindness. Thus: 'Whether sex acts are gay or straight, coupled or in groups, naked or in underwear, commercial or free, with or without video', these issues should not be the basis of ethical concerns. In her revision, the brick walls would no longer be structured around pious perceptions of 'blessed' sexual unions and their demonized alternatives, but along the spectrum of mutuality and consideration on the one side, to unwarranted force and abuse on the other. Reconciling this with the beliefs of those alarmed by lesbian biblical hermeneutics will be an uphill struggle so long as the only acceptable Christian theology is a vanilla 'decent'

Christian theology, fearful of the fruitier flavours that Althaus-Reid brings out of the closet. Pioneering the way forward, she goes to the sexual minorities and locates the faces of God that are there revealed. In so doing, she deconstructs heterosexist constructs that have been at the foundation of Western theologies and opens our minds to who and what God can be, thereby freeing God to surprise us and bring novelty into our spiritual lives. 'Why can we not speak imaginatively of God the faggot?' she asks on pages 67–9 of *Indecent Theology* and she answers, because 'we cannot see the divine outside the reductive structures of a systematic Sexual Theology which knows little about love outside decent regulatory systems of controllable sexual categories'.[23]

Reconciliation? Yes, it is an important part of my work, but there is a long way to go.

Conclusion

Many lesbians are still driven out of their religious homes, or choose not to pursue any reconciliation with religious organizations seen to be irredeemably homophobic. Some choose to stay and fight. For those who have the endurance to stay there is a need for a method of interpreting the Bible that doesn't hide one's loving and genderqueer-ness from God and God's representatives, but finds within it resources that enable a bold and courageous stance, a way of dancing on the edge.[24] This means dealing with the texts of terror and their deployment within the modern world, but also finding a joyful, exuberant affirmation in scriptures.

However, the work of lesbian biblical hermeneutics is not just for those who stay and fight, it offers a positive contribution to confronting that 'attitudinal nexus' Russell and Bohan refer to, for if reconciliation work is to take place it will involve change and transformation of the homonegative 'fog' that we *all* inhale. Acknowledging that 'all participate in homonegating processes' means that, significantly, 'we can all equally participate in its dismantling'.[25] I believe I am doing my part in this and would call upon those who currently stand on the other side of the road to put aside their fears of beasts lying in wait and dare to see how it looks over here.

Notes

1. Deryn Guest, *When Deborah Met Jael: Lesbian Biblical Hermeneutics*, London: SCM Press, 2005.
2. Kimeron Hardin writes of 'gay and lesbian clients [who] . . . were constantly told, "God despises you," or that they were "sentenced to hell" for having an attraction to someone of the same sex. These messages became a deep-seated scar for many of them, making them feel that they did not deserve spiritual nurturing or even feel any joy at all' (*The Gay Self-Esteem Book: A Guide to Loving Ourselves*, Oakland CA: New Harbinger Pubs Inc., 1999, p. 172). Among various solutions, Hardin suggests bibliotherapy and supplies a list of supportive literature on pages 202–3. Deana F. Morrow's advice for 'helping professionals' is similarly that they locate 'a reading list of lesbian-affirming theology and spirituality' ('Cast into the wilderness: the impact of institutionalized religion on lesbians', *Journal of Lesbian Studies*, 7, (2003), pp. 109–23, p. 120). The lesbian biblical hermeneutics project is part of such affirming work.
3. See Deryn Guest, 'Lamentations', in Deryn Guest, Robert E. Goss, Mona West, Tom Bohache (eds), *The Queer Bible Commentary*, London: SCM Press, 2006, pp. 394–411, and 'Liturgy and Loss: A Lesbian Perspective on using Psalms of Lament in Liturgy', in Stephen Burns, Michael N. Jagessar and Nicola Slee (eds), *The Edge of God: New Liturgical Texts and Contexts in Conversation*, London: Epworth Press, forthcoming.
4. On understanding lesbian identities as 'becoming' see Christina K. Hutchins, 'Unconforming Becomings: The Significance of Whitehead's Novelty and Butler's Subversion for the Repetitions of Lesbian Identity and the Expansion of the Future', in Ellen T. Armour and Susan M. St Ville (eds), *Bodily Citations: Religion and Judith Butler*, [Gender, Theory and Religion], New York: Columbia University Press, 2006, pp. 120–56.
5. Vivienne C. Cass's essay ('Homosexual Identity Formation: A Theoretical Model', *Journal of Homosexuality*, 4 [1979], pp. 219–35) was influential, and there has been an outpouring of stage theory during the 1980s–90s (though there is a much smaller corpus of material for bisexual or transgender development; see R. C. Fox, 'Bisexual Identities', in Anthony R. D'Augelli, Charlotte J. Patterson (eds), *Lesbian, Gay and Bisexual Identities over the Lifespan: Psychological Perspectives*, New York: Oxford University Press, 1995, pp. 48–86 and A. H. Devor, 'Witnessing and Mirroring: A Fourteen-Stage Model of Transsexual Identity Formation', *Journal of Gay and Lesbian Psychiatry*, 8, (1/2), pp. 41–67). Recent contributors to the debate note that the idea of linear progression is deeply flawed: development can be spiral, people can skip stages, and most models are dogged by insufficient engagement with difference. Useful reviews of stage theories include Chad M. Mosher, 'The Social Implications of

Sexual Identity Formation and the Coming-Out Process: A Review of the Theoretical and Empirical Literature', *The Family Journal: Counseling and Therapy for Couples and Families*, 9, (20), (2001), pp. 164–73; M. Eliason and Robert Schope, 'Shifting Sands or Solid Foundation? Lesbian, Gay, Bisexual, and Transgender Identity Formation', in Ilan H. Meyer and Mary E. Northridge (eds), *The Health of Sexual Minorities: Public Health Perspectives on Lesbian, Gay, Bisexual and Transgender Populations*, New York: Springer-Verlag New York Inc., 2007, pp. 3–26, and for a review specifically geared to lesbian identities see C. Kitzinger and S. Wilkinson, 'Transitions from Heterosexuality to Lesbianism: The discursive production of Lesbian Identities', *Developmental Psychology*, 31 (1) (1995), pp. 95–104.
6. Paula C. Rust, 'Finding a Sexual Identity and Community: Therapeutic Implications and Cultural Assumptions in Scientific Models of Coming Out', in Esther D. Rothblum & Lynn A Bond, *Preventing Heterosexism and Homophobia*, California, London & New Delhi: Sage Publications, 1996, pp. 87–123, here 92–3). Leanne McCall Tigert's (limited) data highlighted a repeated significant psychological theme 'of loss and the fear of loss', not just of losing one's job, safety, or family but also one's church home (*Coming Out Through Fire: Surviving the Trauma of Homophobia*, Cleveland, Ohio: United Church Press, 1999, p. 37). See also her earlier work (*Coming Out While Staying In: Struggles and Celebrations of Lesbians, Gays ad Bisexuals in the Church*, Cleveland Ohio: United Church Press, 1996, p. 118) together with that of Morrow ('Cast into the Wilderness') and Alison Webster, *Found Wanting: Women, Christianity and Sexuality*, London: Cassell, 1995.
7. Indicator words for internalized homophobia include 'impaired', 'negative', or 'distorted' which 'encourages the view that LGBT people are viewed as having contracted the illness dubbed internalized homophobia' (G. M. Russell and J. S. Bohan, 'The Case of Internalized Homophobia: Theory and/as Practice', *Theory Psychology*, 16 (2006), pp. 343–66, p. 346).
8. Russell and Bohan, 'Internalized Homophobia', p. 351.
9. *Ibid.*
10. Russell and Bohan 'Internalized Homophobia', p. 350.
11. *Ibid.*
12. Russell and Bohan, 'Internalized Homophobia', p. 352.
13. As I was writing this essay, BBC Radio 4 aired a programme on the Bible and homosexuality as part of its regular 'Beyond Belief' slot (broadcast on 30 July 2007). In the course of the debate both responses were identifiable. Thus any overt lesbian or gay interpretation of the David and Jonathan stories was quickly cast aside. These characters might have been close to one another but any sexual relationship is the result of unwarranted exegesis. Rev. Colin Coward, Director of 'Changing Attitudes', was later asked whether acceptance of incest

or adultery would follow from acceptance of homosexuality. He, at least, escaped the beasts.
14. Robert E. Goss, 'Insurrection of the Polymorphously Perverse: Queer Hermeneutics', in J. Michael Clark and Robert E. Goss, (eds.), A Rainbow of Religious Studies, Texas: Monument Press, 1996, pp. 9–31, p. 22.
15. *Ibid.* emphasis added.
16. For a good example of this see Daniel Patte's essay on how readings of Rom. 1:26–7 produce very different results depending upon one's interpretative framework and choices ('Can one be critical without being autobiographical?', in I. R. Kitzberger, (ed.), *Autobiographical Biblical Criticism: Between Text and Self*, Leiden: Deo, 2002, pp. 34–59.
17. Rebecca Alpert, 'Finding Our Past. A Lesbian Interpretation of the Book of Ruth', in Judith A. Kates and Gail Twersky Reimer (eds), *Reading Ruth: Contemporary Women Reclaim a Sacred Story*, New York: Ballantine Books, 1994, pp. 91–6.
18. See Rebecca Alpert, *Like Bread on the Seder Plate: Jewish Lesbians and the Transformation of Tradition*, New York: Columbia University Press, 1997 and S. Tamar Kamionkowski, 'Psalms', in Deryn Guest, Robert E. Goss, Mona West, Tom Bohache (eds), *The Queer Bible Commentary*, London: SCM Press, pp. 304–24.
19. Gayle Rubin, 'Thinking Sex: Notes for a Radical Theory of the Politics of Sexuality', in Carol S. Vance, (ed.), *Pleasure and Danger: Exploring Female Sexuality*, London: Pandora, 1992, pp. 267–319, p. 281, 282.
20. Rubin, 'Thinking Sex' p. 282.
21. *Ibid.* DMZ refers to de-militarized zone.
22. Rubin, 'Thinking Sex', p. 283.
23. Marcella Althaus-Reid, *Indecent Theology. Theological Perversions in Sex, Gender and Politics*, London and New York: Routledge, 2001.
24. This felicitous phrase is used by Richard Holloway (*Dancing on the Edge: Making Sense of Faith in a Post-Christan Age*, London: Harper Collins, 1997) and can be found in the inspiring poetry of Rosie Miles in Geoffrey Duncan, *Courage to Love: An Anthology of Inclusive Worship Material*, London: Darton Longman & Todd, 2002, pp. 78–9).
25. Russell and Bohan, 'Internalized Homophobia', p. 361.

Letter to a Young Gay Catholic

JAMES ALISON

Carissimo,

What a privilege it is to be given the chance to write to you! So much so that I would like to savour the word 'you' for a little bit and ask you to consider what a novelty it is, how open-ended a form of address.

How often have you ever been addressed by the word 'you' in a Catholic publication? I don't mean the word 'you' in the weak sense as when advertisements ask 'Have you considered a vocation to be a priest or sister?' Because those advertisements don't really mean 'you'. They really mean 'someone who is like you in every way, but happens not to be gay, or at least is good at hiding it'. Normally whenever there is a discussion about matters gay in Catholic publications, the style very quickly becomes stiff, and a mysterious 'they' appears. This 'they' seems to inhabit another planet from the one you inhabit. Whoever is talking about 'they' is, in fact, on another planet, one where a strange lack of oxygen makes it impossible to use the pronouns 'I', 'you', 'we'. If someone does start to use those pronouns, you quickly sense that the only thing that gives them the freedom to do so is that they are heterosexual and are honest enough to say that they don't really understand what it's all about.

You may have tried to talk informally about being a gay Catholic to a priest, or even a bishop, whom your gaydar has picked up as likely to be 'family', and you will have noticed how, with all their desire to be friendly, a hidden check comes into their voice. A kind of internal restraining order means that when they say 'you', you can pick up that the 'I' that is speaking has moved into a mode of masking, has become somehow official, and the 'you' who is being spoken to is not being breathed into being, but somehow designated as 'to be handled with extreme caution'. There is a 'but' hovering in the background of the voice which speaks as loud as anything they say, because the 'but' says 'you, but not as you are'.

So here you are, reading a Catholic publication, part of that huge and fantastic worldwide communication network which is one of the joys of being a Catholic, and somehow something new is being allowed to happen. For you, a Catholic who happens to be gay (whatever that means), are being addressed as 'you' by a Catholic who is able to say 'I am a Catholic who happens to be gay, whatever that means'. *I* am being allowed to talk to *you*, who are aware of having the beginnings of a life-story in which being gay plays a part. And I am being offered the chance to speak to you not in an official capacity but as a brother, a brother with something of a life story which includes being an openly gay man. I am being given the chance of addressing you from the same level as you are, as one who doesn't know better than you about who you are, and doesn't even know very much about who I am. Yet a novelty has occurred. It has become possible in a mainstream Catholic publication for the word 'you' to be pronounced in an open-ended way, one which I hope will resonate creatively in your being, by an 'I' whose tone has been inflected and stretched through living as an openly gay man within the Catholic Church.

Like all cowards, when I was faced with the privilege of taking part in this communication my first reaction was to run away. For a privilege is a responsibility. And there is something particularly awesome about this privilege, since there is only One who can address you as 'You' in such a way as to call your 'I' into being without displacing you or bullying you. And that is Our Lord himself. And he won that ability by going through death so as to be able to speak you and me into being and give us both an 'I' not run by death and its fear. There is nothing cheap about being able to talk to another as 'you' in such a way that it calls into being.

When the teaching officials of our Church remember themselves – which is usually when they are on the defensive – they point out that what they call the 'magisterium' can never be a substitute for conscience but can only be a voice alongside your own, at the same level as your own, as subject to the breath of Our Lord as your own. A voice prompting you, counselling you, helping you to form your conscience, and never one drowning you out so that you take on its voice instead of going through the hard work of allowing yourself to be given your own.

They are quite right in this. And I have no right to be any less careful than the magisterium is when talking to you. You see, the difference between my attempt to address you as 'you' and that of the priest or the bishop with the 'check', the glowering 'but', in the back of his voice, is not that he is a hypocrite and I am not, that he is constrained, and I am not. No, I am just as much a hypocrite as he, and I am just as constrained. There is a 'but' in the back of my voice too, though it is not applied to you. However, it would be dishonest if I were to pretend that loving the Church as a gay man had not left some wear in the back of my voice. The realities which cause the priest or bishop to talk to you in a tense and unnatural way are the same realities as force me to think long and hard about how I am to talk to you. And I dread to think how inadequate you would find me if you could talk to me face to face rather than encounter me through this mask which I am spinning with words, words which I can correct, and edit, and change before they reach you.

If there is a difference between the tone of voice with which I am speaking to you and the one you are accustomed to hearing, it is largely one of accident, or grace, depending on how you interpret it. And yes, *you* will have to interpret it, *you* will have to decide whether I who am addressing you as 'you' am able to do so only because of some slip-up, some crack in the system, or whether there is something of the Shepherd in this unauthorized voice which is speaking to you, something of the Shepherd, whose voice you know, and of which you are not afraid. I can lay no claim to being a channel of that voice myself. None of us can. We can hope to be used, or to be in preparation for being used. However only those whom each of us addresses can perceive who it is, what mixture of voices it is, that comes singing through our airwaves.

If there is a difference, then let me confess, it comes from an act of stubbornness, of defiance on my part. A refusal to believe something. That is the 'but' in the back of my voice. '... But the God who is revealed to us in Jesus could not possibly treat that small portion of humanity which is gay and lesbian to a double-bind in the way the Church has come to do. Could not possibly say "I love you, but only if you become something else"; or "Love your neighbour, but in your case, not as yourself, but as if you were someone else"; or "Your love is too dangerous and destructive, find something else to do"'. And for a Catholic, an act of stubbornness or defiance doesn't seem an awfully good place to start. It sounds satanic. Unless of course this refusal to believe something is empowered by such a strong sense of someone's goodness that you know that you would be seriously offending them if you were to believe them capable of acting in the way that is imputed to them.

You can imagine, as I can, a wife refusing to believe in the guilt which a duly appointed court, and a jury of his peers, imputes to her husband concerning some financial dishonesty. All the evidence seems to point in the same direction, but still the wife stubbornly and defiantly refuses to believe that her husband could have done this thing, even when he himself sometimes wavers in his own defence, maybe so as to let her off the strain of having to support him. In some stories this affair will end with new evidence, or a shift in circumstance, completely exonerating the husband, and the wife will be shown to have been right in refusing to allow her faith in her husband's goodness to be contaminated by public calumny. In other stories, there will be no happy resolution, and a generation of bystanders will consider the wife to be a pathetic figure, unhinged from reality, so deep in denial as to be unable to accept that her husband was a crook.

Well, I don't want to pull the wool over your eyes! I am that stubborn and defiant wife, and the story hasn't ended yet. Neither do I know, nor do you know, whether my refusal to believe that God could possibly treat gay and lesbian people in the way that the village elders and the local court say he does, is a refusal born of faith in a love which will turn out to be true, or is simply a sign of my delusional flight into unreality. Those who speak to you with a check in their voice know perfectly well that it is one or the other, and they are taking your safety seriously, not wishing to embark you on such a risky journey.

No, I don't want to pull the wool over your eyes. For to invite you into the place of that defiant wife, and therefore the place of vulnerability and uncertainty until the story is brought to an end, is not something I do easily. It is a frightening place. For I cannot offer you a resolution. I do not know whether it isn't an act of arrogance on my part which says 'it is better to dare to go through the place of being afraid that being gay may simply be a lie, a form of self-deception leading nowhere, trusting that the Spirit of God will dissipate the fear, reveal the fear as a mirage, enable me to grow childlike as I face down the fear; better that, than to cling to the opinion that the fear is for our safety, protecting us from an abyss of meaninglessness, and so allow ourselves to be guided by the prudent "no" of our Church tradition'.

You see, I don't despise the prudent 'no' any longer. I used to. I used to hate the cowardice, the two-facèdness and the lies. But now that I realise the cost of stepping out of that, I also realise how careful I must be when addressing you. For which of us can tell whether some petulant desire for heroism might not be pulling our strings, rather than the breath of the Lord saying '*Duc in altum!*' – 'Put out into the deep!' (Luke 5.4). There where the prudent think there are no fish to be caught, no humans worth loving with equality of heart, only a swirling of messy and unrescuable desires. The cost of stepping out of the protective 'no!', of believing that someone might be addressing me as 'You' without that dreaded 'but', is finding myself naked before the Spirit and more vulnerable than ever to my own self-deception. And the only resolution will be when the catch begins to come in, and that may not be in my lifetime, or in yours.

No, I don't want to pretend that being an openly gay Catholic is something easy or obvious. It isn't. For a start, merely the fact of your wanting to read a letter like this at all is a sign of how many obstacles you must have overcome already. You may have faced hatred and discrimination in your own country, from family members, at school, at the hands of legislators eager for cheap votes, through shrieking newspaper headlines that sear your soul, and in the glare of which you are speechless in your own defence. And you've probably noticed that at the very best, the Church which calls itself, and is, your Holy Mother has kept silent about the hatred and the fear. While all too often its spokesmen will have lowered themselves to the level of second-rate politicians, lending voice to hate while claiming that they are standing up for love. The very fact that, through and in the midst of, and despite, all these hateful voices, you should have heard the voice of the Shepherd calling you into being of his flock is already a miracle far greater than you know, preparing you for a work more subtle and delicate than those voices could conceive.

You will share in all the contempt which the modern world has for the Catholic Church by virtue of holding firm to the faith you have been given – you will be considered as having little of worth to offer. And by virtue of being a Catholic you will always be on the brink of being considered something of a traitor to whatever project your contemporaries seek to build. No surprise there: that goes with the turf. However you will face something in addition, for you will be considered something of a traitor within the Church as well. 'Not quite one of us'. And certainly not someone who can publicly represent the Church, be a visible part of the sign which leads to salvation. And how could it be otherwise? For if being gay is a defect in creation, as is held, then the only sign of grace attaching to being gay would be the removal of being gay from what makes you or me to be.

Do not be surprised, then, that they will be considered loyal and trustworthy who pursue every conceivable psychological false lead with a view to finding scientific backing for the claim that being gay is a pathology. They will receive approval as 'a sign of contradiction', of not yielding to the spirit of the age. While you will be considered a bad Catholic, if a Catholic at all. For, long after the evangelical groups which gave birth to 'reparative therapy' and the 'ex-gay' movement have moved on, and their leaders apologised for leading people astray, such ideas will find Catholic backers and supporters, since they flatter current Church teaching. But don't be afraid of those ideas, and don't hate their propagators. They are our brothers. The very fact that these brothers understand that if the Church's teaching is true it must have some basis in the discoverable realm of nature means that ultimately it is the evidence of what is true in that realm which will set us free. It will be bigger than what either you, or I, or they, can guess right now, and it will set us all free.

But what of the long 'meanwhile'? For you, called by your name, just as for me, who am learning to receive an 'I', being Catholic implies a vocation to some sort of ministry, some sort of creative acting out, some sort of public imitation of the life and death of Our Lord. So I don't want to pretend: you will find yourself developing a ministry, as I find myself developing one, without any public backing from Church authority. It will be as if you did not exist. You will have to learn to live in the silence of being neither approved of, nor even disapproved of. You will fall out of the gaze of men, and if you are anything like me, desperate for an approving glance, you will experience this as a form of dying. For each of us is given to be who we are through the gaze of others, and we respond to that gaze, allowing it to give us who we are to be, and we behave accordingly. So, to drop through the floor into a space where there is no gaze, no approval, not even any disapproval, is a terrifying and risky business.

For of course, I may have dropped through the floor into the space where there is no gaze because I have become hermetic in my own pride and self-deception. In which case I will never find a gaze, but will dance to the rhythm of that deception, thinking myself very holy and special until death comes. Or, if I am being led by the Spirit of God, the place where there is no gaze may turn into the space where I am found in the regard of God. And this will be experienced by me as a *'nada'*, a nothing, all around, and only others may perceive that there is an 'I' being called into being by One whose eyes I cannot see, but who can see me, a breath I cannot feel, and yet upon which I am being held. And of course, others will not necessarily understand what they see coming into being any more than I will.

What might you be embarking on? Let me give you an analogy. I don't know whether you are old enough to remember the Cold War? Or indeed whether the Cold War had enough of an incidence in your part of the world to have made much of an impression on you as you grew up. One of the spin-offs of the Cold War was a literary and cinematic genre of spy stories, tales of intrigue and underground life waged (in the worst cases) by goodies against baddies and in somewhat rarer, better, cases by morally ambiguous people on both sides of the NATO/Eastern Bloc divide.

Try to imagine yourself an agent for one or the other side – from my perspective it is easiest to imagine myself as a Western agent buried deep in communist lands. Now imagine that long ago you received your instructions from the head of the agency which is to 'run' you, and were given appointed 'handlers' for your mission. So, confident that you were being backed up by them, you plunged into your work, starting to build up community, small signs of the kingdom you serve, deep in enemy territory. Then imagine that something weird happens, there is something of a coup within the agency that sent you out, a policy shift, and all the people who had 'handled' you, knew you, and prepared you, are quietly retired. So you find yourself with no direct line to anyone back at the agency. You are deep underground, and you are suddenly without cover, without back up, without resources, without even recognition. So much so that the new agents sent out by the agency don't even know of your existence, and would probably heartily disapprove since if you are who you say you are, then you are part of an older and currently discredited approach to the 'enemy territory' in which you have long gone underground.

And of course, there are people in the agency who might know about you, but they can no longer afford to say so. For to be seen to have contact with you would put into jeopardy their own standing in the agency. In short, you find yourself having become a non-person. 'Doesn't exist on our books, Madam' is the answer given to any enquiry at HQ made by someone foolish enough to have claimed to have known you. Plausible deniability is the lubricating oil by which the agency works.

What are you to do? You are still loyally at work, loving the project for which you were originally sent out. But communications have become seriously patchy. You can hear on the Radio the official pronouncements of the agency. You can read between the lines the 'real' meaning of what is being said, but you do not exist, you have no line of communication back to HQ, you are a no one. So, do you allow your anger and resentment at your treatment by the agency to cause you to give up working on the project for which you were originally called and trained? Or do you so love the project that you are prepared to love the agency which now hates you, confident that eventually, things will work out? Loving the agency when it loves you is easy enough, but loving it even through the time when it disowns you? Now there is the finger of God!

This is where I would urge you, as I urge myself, often with a fainting spirit, to see the privilege of what we have. Yes, there is a communication black-out with an HQ which can only talk about a 'they' and never address 'you'; yes, they either don't know of our existence, or need plausible deniability for their own sakes, but meanwhile here, deep in enemy territory we can carry on building not just a wee little corner of something defensive, but the Catholic Church itself – the full thing, the whole whack. And curiously, with less interference from busybodies than would be the case if the lines of communication were up. So, do we dare to have our love stretched by building without approval, as we wait longingly for the day when some Berlin Wall comes down, and communication is restored? Can you take responsibility for that? Can you persevere?

'¡*Esto va para largo* . . .' 'This is going to be a long haul!' – that was the sage advice to me of one of my formators, one of my handlers, who in addition to being a gay man is an historian. He was telling me, as I am telling you, that the process of adjustment to truth in this sphere is going to take a long, long time. And it will only happen if people like you and me are prepared to love the project and not mind the turmoil in the agency, if we are generous in giving the handlers time to summon up the bravery to seek us out and talk to us as co-workers. One of the things that will keep us going is that we can keep returning to those weird cold-war meeting places, the drop-boxes of spy communication, where very quietly, from beneath ancient texts and through bread and wine, our original formator and our first handler, the One who first enlivened the project for us, will whisper courage and strength and perseverance into us, while the current agency boys run distraction, creating senseless noise, but fail finally to quench the ancient code.

Who knows, my friend, whether this opportunity for communication will be repeated? Who knows whether this is just a blip in the ether, whether the blockers of the Catholic radio waves will manage to prevent further open exchange between a Catholic 'I' and a Catholic 'you' both of whom happen to be gay? Or whether there is not some thaw in the ecclesiastical permafrost, and talk will get much, much easier? One way or another, let me tell you what I have discovered in my years underground in enemy territory: you are not alone, and His promises are true.

with a big hug
from your brother,

James

II. THEOLOGICAL FORUM

Reading the Signs of the Times:
Concilium – Partner in a Common Journey

FELIX WILFRED

Reading the signs of the times is something very invigorating. It makes the journey of life exalting, because new possibilities and challenges appear on the horizon. But it is a difficult task too. Because the reading happens in a world of ambiguities with too many confusing signs: globalization with its opportunities and dangers; hegemony of market forces and consequent culture of consumerism; endemic poverty and oppression; mass-migration with the inherent possibility of cross-cultural and economic enrichment, which, at the same time, gives rise to xenophobia; the escalating terrorism in every part of the globe expressing a deep sense of discontentment with the established systems and international order; ambiguous nuclearization of nations – these signs co-exist with a deep and persistent search for peace with justice; democratization that facilitates participation of people in all areas of life; longing for new forms of community; emergence of the periphery to the fore; the visibility and force of new social movements to bring about transformation.

Identity is one of the major signs of the times. It is also an issue around which some of the more serious problems confronting humanity today become crystallized. What is most worrying is the fact that the ambiguity surrounding identity and its construction has become a source of conflict and violence worldwide. Identity can kill as much as it can enliven life and infuse confidence. Fundamentalism of every colour and hue and ethnicity can be traced to unresolved identity-questions. Peace, harmony, and justice are, therefore, inextricably related to the approach human beings adopt to resolve the issue of identities.

The issue has many facets: at one level, the question could be described as an ambiguous conflict between affirmation and negation of identities. Affirmation could mean either a move toward consolidation of power, as for example when Samuel Huntington, in his book *Who Are We? The Challenges to America's National Identity*, calls for a recovery and assertion of the Protestant identity of his country. On the other hand, identity-assertion is often a means to gain the dignity and rights a people have been denied, as for example when the *Dalits* ('Untouchables') of India, the *Indios* of Latin America, and the Aboriginals of Australia assert their identity. This latter type of assertion calls for a shift from the centre to the margins. It challenges the imposition of identities on the basis of tradition and conventional power bases. Earlier, the centres claimed to possess true identity and arrogated their right to define the identity of the other. Today there is a strong movement to challenge such claims.

There are some positive signs emerging as to how we need to tackle this major issue. One clear line of conviction that promises a lot of hope is that we need to cross borders of every kind – cultural, national, ideological, disciplinary, or religious – and overcome the syndrome of singular identity and recognize that in reality there are multiple layers of identity. There is the urgent need to build up the values and attitudes necessary to enable negotiation of borders, which will help to redefine one's identity in relationship to the other – a great enrichment – or to discover the self through a journey across borders and boundaries – an exciting experience full of surprises. Yet another sign of hope is the convergence toward the creation of a world community as a spiritual project calling forth a different set of values and attitudes than the ones identified with globalization

The agenda of identities poses mighty challenges for Christianity, both in terms of redefining its own identity by forging new relationships across borders, and in terms of contributing to resolve the dilemmas humanity is facing with the question of identity, which has its own specific configuration and contours in different contexts. All this certainly is an invitation for a rethinking and redefining the nature and role of theology.

In one sense, the issue of gender exemplifies in its most basic and radical form the question of identity. Down through the ages, the fullness of being human has been appropriated and defined by the male. This illegitimate monopolizing of the human – belonging equally to man and woman – by the male alone is the reason why women are relegated to the margins and their identity defined as mere bodies incapable of thinking, acting, and being themselves. Thanks to the feminist movement and to women's negotiation of borders between the domestic and the public space, humanity is being challenged to redefine itself and grow toward greater wholeness.

New ethical and moral questions confronting humanity are yet another sign of the times. The rapid developments in every segment of life have also thrown up new and unprecedented ethical dilemmas. The novelty and speed of the new developments in science and technology have had their social and cultural repercussions, the most obvious of which is the glaring imbalance in sharing of the resources of the world, its goods and services, and the disparity in availability of opportunities. A striking fact is that ethical response has not kept pace with these developments, nor has it been able to convincingly address the most intriguing moral questions and dilemmas of our times.

There is also the imbalance caused by the use of calculative reason in studying and controlling nature, the laws of its workings, and the application of these in the field of very complex technologies. These developments with the help of calculative reason have not been synchronized with the development of moral reason that would ensure justice in inter-human relationships and with ecological reason – if I may use the term – which will integrate the human development within sustainable limits and not disrupt the rhythm of nature. Moreover, explorations in genetic and biological fields have opened up new questions so radical that they call for a revision of conventional understanding of the human and of nature.

As for religions, their traditional role as moral teachers has undergone an erosion of credibility, not only owing to the gap between the ideals they project and the actual situation but also, often, because of their failure in intervening effectively in defence of the poor and the weaker ones. There are other moral agencies such as new social movements (ecological movements, human rights movements, and so on) that are bringing a new moral consciousness to humanity. One of the great realizations of Vatican Council II was that the Church does not have solutions to all the problems and questions assailing our world. The openness this entails and the dialogue it calls for with the world remain permanent features of the praxis of faith today and therefore of all theologies. It places Church, faith, and theology on a common journey. This journey involves the crossing of many identities, borders and boundaries.

Concilium understands itself today as being on the way, and on a journey. The publication of the journal of the same name is the expression of a commitment to respond to the signs and challenges of our times. It is to assist the community of believers to understand the Church and faith in such a way that it can be *an* active participant in the search for responses that assail the human family today and become an agent of unity, peace, justice and reconciliation. The fact that *Concilium* still remains, perhaps, the most widely subscribed theological journal in the world is a sign that its contributions respond to the need for a faith-reflection in response to the signs of the times. It is also an indication of the earnestness with which the community of theologians around the journal prepare the various issues year after year.

The fact that *Concilium* has elected a president from a developing country is itself is a clear message of the journey it has made across borders and boundaries. The decision of the body of theologians represented in *Concilium* to locate the secretariat of the journal in Madras, India, also shows how *Concilium* has tried to read the signs of the times and construct a new identity in response to changing times. With these changes, *Concilium* as a theological journal hopes to pursue the path that lies ahead and continue in a creative way its service to the people of God and to the world.

Humanae Vitae:
A Global Reassessment after Forty Years

(A) Considerations beyond the Birth-Control Controversy

DIETMAR MIETH

There has been much discussion of the encyclical *Humanae Vitae* in Catholic moral theology. It is also constantly cited as an obvious general point of reference in critical comments on the Church in the media. In fact the encyclical has seriously affected not only moral theology but dogmatic theology, and not least of all the magisterial proclamation of the Church.

Nevertheless, *Humanae Vitae* has also proved to be a ground-breaking encyclical by proffering a view of love as the meaning of marriage, as distinct if not separate from fertility as its purpose. This position was reinforced by *Familiaris consortio* (1981). The continuing aspect calling for criticism was the prohibition of means of birth control (not only of abortion). In respect of this prohibition, however, the Church appealed to the continuity of its authority and to its conception of natural law.[1] Consequently, the extent to which the Church's magisterial authority was indeed applicable became just as much a point of contention as the type of appeal to natural law that was involved here. From the viewpoint of Tübingen, Hans Küng's critique of the claim to infallibility and of the supporting argumentation was the high point of one dispute, and the foundation of a Catholic school of 'autonomous morality' by Alfons Auer and Franz Böckle was the high point of the other. Episcopal conferences (in Switzerland, Austria, and Germany, for instance) referred to the doctrine of the conscience of the faithful. There was also repeated discussion of the fact that the teaching on birth control was not accepted by the faithful,[2] and from conviction not weakness. The question at issue here was not only the function of conscience but that of the *sensus fidelium* in moral formation in the Catholic Church.

In the present instance, however, I am not concerned with the debate provoked by the Church's ruling, which carried on until the discussion of the encyclical *Veritatis Splendor*.[3] Instead the question is much more one of a general nature: that of the respects in which (in my opinion) the process has led to changes in Christian ethics. The second question is that of the prospects for the future in view of these changes.

Especially in the ways in which the magisterium has made it a yardstick of theologians' loyalty to the Church, *Humanae Vitae* has proved a spur to European and, to a considerable degree, to American moral theologians' reinterpretation of natural law as an autonomous law and right of reason. It has also prompted them to try to align themselves with Aquinas in the course of this project – an attempt which has largely prevailed in spite of intermittent counter-arguments.[4] The form of autonomy in question was neither self-determination, discretion, and free decision (in contradistinction to the 'pro-choice' movement), nor, in spite of certain references to Immanuel Kant, 'personal commitment' in freedom, in the sense of Kantian autonomy, but rather the autonomous rationality of reality, or the autonomy of an interpretation of the true nature of creation when that interpretation is a process open to reason. It is characteristic of the natural-law tradition that this autonomous source of knowledge should never be subsumed in some form of Christomonism and in an ecclesiomonism derived from it.[5] This viewpoint is still discernible in Catholic social doctrine even though, there too, it has not been thought through at any real depth. Accordingly, ethically relevant knowledge should not become apparent primarily as an officially 'christened' form of knowledge. The result has been new instances of relevance for the moral theory of knowledge in a theological context: one of reference to the human and social sciences (a particularly strong tendency in France), but also one of new considerations for philosophical debate, whether as a result of recent interpretations of Kant, or as an outcome of the debate about justice centred on the work of John Rawls.

But the ground covered and gained in this process, and initially in secular social debate too (in Germany, say), was also paid for by certain losses. On the one hand, the ethically relevant approaches of liberation theology and political theologies in general do often rely on a Christological substructure, and thereby ensure that the autonomy of their 'world ethos' (a 'universal ethics' in Alfons Auer's sense) is one subject to natural law and to creation theology. On the other hand, the 'religious turn' has been more inclined to consider the moral force of religions and a possible consensus in the 'world ethos' (or 'global ethics' in Hans Küng's sense). Moreover, as it drifts from secularism into laicism, the world of science, politics, and the media in Europe has paid increasingly less attention to a theologically motivated ethics, however philosophical the cast of its argumentation has been. Because it was located between these two 'stools', 'autonomous morality in a Christian context' prevailed ever more effectively in academic circles in spite of obstacles placed in its way by the magisterium, not least of all because of the distinctions it proffered. Nevertheless, it could prevail socially only if its representatives were able to win an audience by virtue of their practical ethical competence, as distinct from their beliefs.

Humanae Vitae did not bring all this about and is not to be held responsible for it, but some (or quite a lot of) things might well have developed differently without the encyclical. This was also the view of Cardinal Christoph von Schönborn of Vienna when, in a retirement address (of 16 Mar. 2007) for Günter Virt, the Viennese moral theologian, he called the concentration of moral theology (or its increasing tendency to concentrate) on this point 'unfortunate'. I share the opinion of all those who especially deplore the unbending attitude of the magisterium, which has often meant that the prohibition of artificial birth control has had a similar effect to the symbolic hat placed on a stake by the dictatorial Governor Gessler to provoke William Tell, the legendary Swiss folk hero, into active resistance.

According to Cardinal von Schönborn, this conflict prevented a more comprehensive reception of the Second Vatican Council. Attention seemed to be hypnotically focussed on 'autonomy' in *Gaudium et Spes*, whereas other conciliar documents (on revelation and the Church) could also have provided basic principles of moral theology. I think that this outcome does not affect works of moral theology but rather the reception and further effects of these writings.

Of course it is also the responsibility of the magisterium to reduce the tension of this conflict. One bridge between parties could be toleration of condoms in the fight against Aids. Another bridge might be recourse to the doctoral thesis on dogmatic theology (1971) of Cardinal Levada (who now heads the Congregation for the Doctrine of the Faith), in which he maintains that infallibility is not possible in specific questions of natural law.[6] A third bridge might be supplied by reinforcing the doctrine of conscience.[7] A fourth bridge would be to include convictions arising from Christian practice as shown in collected testimonies. To date this has been totally neglected in Rome. There is a plentiful supply of bridges here for a nominated builder of bridges, a *pontifex maximus*. Many such bridges have been proposed in the course of discussion of the encyclical *Veritatis Splendor*.

A relevant anecdote seems appropriate here. In 1989, after the 'Cologne Declaration', when theologians all over the world had also protested on account of the problems between the magisterium and moral theology, one of my associated experiences was a discussion with eighty Polish priests in Katowice about the birth-control ruling. I told them about a Roman prelate who, while hearing a private confession, said that the pill was permissible in an extreme case cited during that confession. (In this extreme case, the mother had already had three children, the next pregnancy would endanger her health, and the 'safe period' could not be used.) But the Polish priests were not interested in approval or refusal in an individual case, or in this exposition of a confessor's discretion. They all wanted a general ruling.

This brings me to my prospect: the brief of the Aids commission which the Pope has asked to examine the Church's teaching should be extended. (More on this below.) Or the new challenges posed by the use of embryos should make it clear where specifically the line is to be drawn: at the preservation of human life after conception. We are faced with a schizoid situation when the Church supports this line in the case of political influences (in Italy, say), but attacks moral theologians whose stance is actually located a long way behind the same line.

Forty years of non-acceptance of a prohibition that goes into very considerable detail should suffice to consider a revision. It would certainly be possible to retain what some liberation theologians and others have called the 'prophetic' aspects of *Humanae Vitae* as against a total (and not merely partial) dominance of the love relationship by the planning mentality and by the increasing technologization of reproduction.

Of course we could also say that ultimately *Humanae Vitae* is like an island on whose reefs various waves have broken and courageous vessels have capsized in attempts to get ashore and cultivate the island differently, but which has now been circumvented by following routes that have become familiar in the meantime. We soon forget what we find irrelevant. Among young Christians, including women theologians, the agitation has died down. *Humanae Vitae* no longer concerns them or has anything to do with their actual behaviour. That does not mean that it has ceased to be a subject for further discussion among moral theologians. But the number of those who pay it any attention is rapidly diminishing.

From the viewpoint of moral theology, however, there is certainly a point in examining how nowadays a philosophically-based rational morality posits *de facto* limits that it would not need to establish *de jure*, if it did not require precisely ethics itself to dispense with more far-reaching questions about the meaning of human existence. In the course of its campaigns for justice and human rights, philosophical moral theory has produced many flourishing gardens as well as individual blooms, but also a certain amount of garbage. But this 'political philosophy' must be distinguished from 'moral philosophy'. The latter tends to meander and has a great number of tributaries that generally run into the secular and pluralist ocean of As You Please. The big questions of human contingency, guilt, and suffering are absent from it. They do not belong within the secular boundaries of a realm where analytical propriety is tested in philosophical laboratories that are almost entirely divorced from the real world and just as minimally concerned with questions of the meaning of life and of undeservedly bestowed happiness. Philosophical moral theory often seems liberal but 'graceless'. Popular philosophers, pundits, and esoteric commentators have their own ways of dealing with this inadequacy. But they never delve into the field of moral responsibility; they let it lie fallow. The more comprehensive anthropology of theological ethics has an advantage here.

The Catholic magisterium is often inclined to accept the use of reason only if it is duly sanctioned, and it lays down rules for the purpose that ordain who carries out this 'christening' procedure, and how and when it should occur. To be sure, in a certain sense theology is also 'christened reason'. But the case of morality is like that of baptism, which can be administered by any Christian, male or female. Theologically speaking, reason, though liberated by creation, is certainly liable to go its own way and be capable of falling into error. But, especially in its modern reflective form, it is also self-critical reason, for there can be no reason without a 'critique of reason'. This critical reason, supported by far-reaching experience, also wanders within and without the Church. Church people can invoke its aid and, indeed, rely on it, but it cannot be enslaved without being perverted. Those who are afraid of the freedom afforded by reason should not practise theology, for they have lost the *Logos*. Of course, those who expect their freedom to bring them everything they hope to achieve are equally deceived. In this respect, I should say, liberation theologians are justified in maintaining that a state of unfreedom that has left the fold of salvation history can also call for the liberation of reason. In the course of history, major philosophical themes and major moral topics must often feature theological emphases with a thrust that is not exclusively but frequently positive.

Many aspects of enlightened humanity have Christian roots, especially in incarnational thought, in the Christological presence in the poor, in a rejection of force, and consequently in the surrender and assumption of sovereignty. Nevertheless, it is essential to distinguish this viewpoint from a normative Christomonism. It is possible to show people that Christ is not heteronomous when he is the essentially decisive power of the religious identity of Christian men and women. Christ dwells exclusively in the doctrinal structure erected by the Church just as little as reason, which bursts the bounds of philosophical laboratories.

Accordingly, a consideration of *Humanae Vitae* forty years on necessarily leads to far-reaching questions of contemporary (moral) theology.

But these are also very specific problems. Therefore the practical moral outcome of the foregoing is: condoms in the case of Aids and an unequivocal protection of life after conception.

Translated by J.G.Cumming

Notes

1. The argument was changed in *Familiaris Consortio*. A primary consideration now was a personal acceptance of one's sexual partner wholly and entirely as a potential father or mother. Nevertheless, this argument was also criticized because of the exaggerated nature of the experiences which it instanced. See D. Mieth, *Geburtenreglung*, Mainz, 1990, p. 166.
2. See especially H. Juros, 'Die Rezeption ethischer Normen', *Theologische Quartalschrift* 169 (1989), 11–122.
3. Cf. D. Mieth (ed.), *Moraltheologie im Abseits? Antwort auf die Enzyklika 'Veritatis Splendor'*, Freiburg im Breisgau, 1994.
4. See, finally, F.-J. Bormann, *Natur als Horizont sittlicher Praxis, Zur handlungstheoretischen Interpretation der Lehre vom natürlichen Sittengesetz des Thomas von Aquin*, Stuttgart, 1999; idem, 'Theologie und "autonome Moral"', *Theologie und Philosophie* 77 (2002), 216–32.
5. It is important to make a distinction between Christomonism and a Christological substantiation of Christian ethics that allows of differentiation in terms of salvation history and values humanity in its own right alongside incarnation.
6. See the abstract of his dissertation at the Gregorian University, Rome 1971. The preface duly offers a response to Hans Küng's *Infallible?* (1970).
7. Cf. B-M. Duffé, 'Conscience morale et Magistère catholique', in: D. Mieth (ed.) *Moraltheologie* (n. 3), pp. 144–76.

(B) Challenges of Updating *Humanae Vitae*

MÁRCIO FABRI DOS ANJOS

Reading *Humanae Vitae* (HV) today certainly leads into many and complex realms. The various questions it raises have been discussed and analyzed since its publication, and each decade has brought new assessments and re-readings. Today, however, we are in a new situation, not because the text of the encyclical has changed but because the contexts in which it applies have changed. One of the necessities for a current re-reading is, therefore, to see how the statements made in the encyclical interact with a changing world. At the same time we must assume that the document has a guiding value: that is, it claims to be an evangelical message to the world, on the subject of contraception.

This provides us with a good basic question for this re-reading: To what extent have the contents of this encyclical conveyed, and do they still convey, this evangelical service to our world? This is my concern in these brief considerations. I am not setting out to provide a synthesis of its historical evolution, which would be very demanding in view of the voluminous bibliography on the subject.[1] Furthermore, we should have to bear in mind that many of HV's contents are repeated in other church documents without it being quoted as such.[2] I merely seek to add some modest personal considerations to add to other *aperçus* of the subject.

I. The challenge of changing realities

There are two types of problems that the encyclical first brought to light: those related to the *facts* of the discovery and use of contraceptives and those related to the values and criteria employed in their *ethical evaluation*. The conjunction of the two gives the encyclical its structure, as well as the prophetic and at the same time polemical aspects of its statements. Divergences in accepting HV's proposal definitely indicate divergences over the values and criteria employed in its ethical evaluation of the *facts*. But this leads to the complex question of the differences in moral understanding that people bring to their perception, analysis, and evaluation of the facts. In the final analysis it could be said that the encyclical sets out to be precisely an evangelical service for forming Christian moral understanding of the matter.

After this brief theoretical note, let us move directly to a closer look at the body of facts of contraception that HV posits at the outset. A first concern would be the biological impact of wide use of contraceptives. Understanding of this impact has become clearer over the years. As Javier Gafo has noted,[3] the Synod on the Family, held in 1980, twelve years after HV, registered a progressive concern with the harmful effects of hormonal contraceptives, with a resultant decline in their use in the wealthy countries. Their scientific evolution since then has perfected the dosage, but even this diminution has not eliminated their harmful side-effects. Worldwide ethical consciousness has gradually seen the need for moderation in the use of technologies and is suggesting more *ecological* ways of living.

A second group of problems revolves around the relational impact of the use of contraceptives. Public policies applied in poor countries, such as in Latin America, impose contraception through 'strong economic pressures, since aid for emergence from underdevelopment was made conditional on the implementation of anti-*natalist* campaigns'.[4] In interpersonal relationships the main impact of contraception falls on women. Statistics from 1994, for example, show that in one region of Brazil 44 percent of women of child-bearing age (fifteen to forty-five) had been sterilized.[5] Such figures have been gradually lowered through government campaigns, such as are currently taking place in Brazil, to encourage and facilitate male sterilization.

Changes related to values and criteria have been evaluated by the magisterium in successive documents, particularly those of John Paul II, the encyclicals *Evangelium Vitae*, *Veritatis Splendor*, and *Fides et Ratio*. These provide a major development of HV on this subject.

II. Acceptance of values and criteria in a changing world

Acceptance of HV has depended, and continues to do so, on the perception of values and criteria with which to make a moral judgment on the use of contraceptives. Let us look at three aspects that involve this framework: theoretical, practical or experiential, and normative.

(a) On the *theoretical aspects* of HV, I am not entering here into discussion on the concept of natural law or on the encyclical's argumentation on the *intrinsic* 'disorder' involved in the use of artificial contraceptives.[6] This aspect of HV has been at the centre of polemic around it, since there were already divergent theories about these concepts at the time of its publication. As is well known, differences were made plain in the two separate reports prepared by the commission of experts who oversaw the preparation for the encyclical. This tension is still present in the Church, as shown in the encyclical *Veritatis Splendor*,[7] published in 1993 and which also caused some problems of reception.[8]

The above is noted simply to show that HV interacted with a very lively theological ambience. Taking stock twenty years after its publication, it was quite widely recorded that a considerable change had taken place in respect of theoretic reference points: 'The overall picture of moral theology has changed profoundly in recent years: [. . .] these have seen the formation of a school that values existence over essence, culture over nature, historicity over immutability, subjectivity over objectivity'.[9] This outpouring of thought is far from being resolved and represents a continual challenge to the encyclical.

(b) *The life-experience of persons* is, from another angle, a great laboratory for constructing moral values and norms. Over twenty years ago I had an interesting dialogue with a penitent who accused himself of using artificial methods of contraception. I asked him what he made of that, before God. He replied that it was absolutely not a sin; nevertheless, he was confessing it because his parents said it was a sin. 'But God understands my situation very well: I already have five children; my wife is ill, and I am not made of iron.' This is one example of how the norms laid down in HV do not reach people's lives with a sufficient degree of conviction. The actual needs in people's lives speak louder in the midst of complex situations, where theories are unable to help.

A *pastoral vision*, from close to people's lives, one that takes account of their needs and goods as they exist in actual situations, generates conclusions that at the very least modify some of the statements of HV. One example would be the use of condoms in preventing the HIV virus. Cardinal Paulo Evaristo Arns, then archbishop of São Paulo, gave an interview in 1995 in which he opined that their use was a 'lesser evil'.[10] More recently, Cardinal Carlo Maria Martini, then archbishop of Milan, professed a similar view, further stressing the challenge posed by married couples protecting one another against the virus: 'Of course the use of prophylactics can in some situations constitute a lesser evil. This is especially the case with spouses one of whom is affected with Aids. This brings an obligation to protect the other partner, who should in any case be able to protect him-/herself'.[11]

Research carried out in 2001 among priests from a poor pastoral district of Rio de Janeiro, on 'what priests say and what they keep quiet about' on sexuality and reproduction, shows this tension between theory and pastoral practice. The priests accepted 'a great gap between what the Church says and how the people live': even a contradiction, since 'the law of the Church here is in direct conflict with the situation'. Faced with this situation, the generalized reaction among the priests interviewed was 'not to ask about these matters'. As for the people, it is becoming rarer and rarer for them to confess on this point.[12]

These tensions in the pastoral sphere are known worldwide and were already present when HV was published. An analysis of the situation made ten years later concluded summarily: 'The patterns of human reproduction are changing, the requirements for religious legitimacy are changing, and the contradiction between the traditional teaching of the Catholic hierarchy and the reproductive behaviour of Catholics is becoming obvious.'[13]

(c) Here consideration of the *normative aspect* seems essential to reflection: faced with such a variety of situations and of moral judgments, what degree of reception of the *normative* aspect of the encyclical has there been? Here too I am not proposing to enter the ring of theoretical debate over the normative value of statements by the magisterium. It is of greater concern to note that reception of HV in the field of pastoral ministry to ordinary people is broadly marked by the idea of a taxing norm that defines the use of 'artificial methods of contraception' as sinful. Various ecclesial groups, of authoritarian stamp, emphasize this prescriptive side, contributing to the encyclical's proposals being seen as a harsh discipline.

This disciplinary side has been shown in official rebukes made to various theologians on matters related to the subject of the encyclical. The research carried out among priests also reveals their fear of speaking out and thereby doing themselves professional damage. So nearly a third of the group mentioned above refused to give interviews on account of 'the difficulty of tackling a controversial subject, surrounded by preconceptions and taboos, and on which many think it best to remain silent'.[14]

Meanwhile, modern times have brought significant changes in the manner of dealing with disciplinary decisions. The very *legitimization* of religious norms, despite the persistence of fundamentalisms, today requires dialogue with subjective perceptions. While on the one hand moral under-

Challenges of Updating Humanae Vitae

standing in the Christian community and each of its individual members cannot be supposed to be well grounded, on the other it is becoming increasing questionable whether the attempt to instruct them through disciplinary methods can be justified.

III. The challenge of updating: viewpoints

We should accept that the encyclical HV, if one looks beyond its polemical aspects, is still relevant in the basic questions it raises. This means that the challenge for Christian moral reflection to provide an evaluative contribution today, as the encyclical does, is now equally valid. In other words, it is worth examining its content in a forward-looking way, in search of what might provide a contemporary evangelical service to the formation of Christian understanding of the matter. Within the limitations of this essay, I should like to choose just three aspects of HV for consideration from the point of view of its updating.

(a) The *prophetic power* of the encyclical in confronting various tendencies of modern Western culture has often been recognized. All over the world, there is abundant written testimony to the influence of instrumental reasoning and individualism in projecting values and criteria for moral action. HV provides sustenance to the courage to seek ethical criteria in an integral vision of *corporeal* and *spiritual* human beings and their relationships. Despite the criticisms of 'biologism' levelled against it, its presentation of the respect due to biological processes remains pertinent, and ecological understanding recognizes this to an extent. From the relational point of view, especially in poor regions of the world, it also stresses the centrality of social responsibility and of justice in relationships involving human reproduction. In short, we can hope for Christian input into an ethical and spiritual environment in which human reproduction is exercised responsibly, and in which its evangelical contribution of justice and generosity will certainly offer a contrast with many present-day tendencies.

(b) But how do we apply justice and generosity to complex relationships in the daily round of interpersonal and social life? From the time of HV this question, already identified by Vatican II,[15] has elicited *different models of theological ethics* in response to it.[16] The several theoretical viewpoints are not really the problem; how to deal with them in ecclesial relationships is. The tensions in this sphere are well known and have led to fear of displaying variance from the official viewpoint of the magisterium, as has been noted above. The impasse will last as long as there is difficulty in progressing dialogue among the various ethical models. The silence from some quarters can only provide a convenient solution, not a meeting on theoretically equal ground.

(c) The gap between the *official teaching* and the *actual practice* of the faithful where the use of contraceptive methods is concerned is perhaps the most important aspect on which a future revision of HV has to concentrate. It is here that the various challenges represented by such a gap converge: (1) it can mean a moving away from the evangelical commitment to justice and generosity in matters of fertility, which would imply a missionary challenge to prophetic proclamation in our times; (2) the gap can be due to the lack of agreement over the criteria and values required for evaluation and moral ruling on the issue; this would present a challenge to dialogue with the reasoning of today's faithful, especially once the temptation to remove the challenge through simple disciplinary imposition has been overcome; (3) it results from a failure to perceive the relationship between the word of God (interpreted by, or based on the encyclical) and the complex realities experienced by people in real life; this is where the challenge, already present in the second aspect, becomes acute in its relationship to the pedagogy of Christian morality designed to assist in forming consciences with a view to responsible behaviour, since in complex situations justice and generosity do not change in substance but need to be expressed in different ways. Such a pedagogical challenge supposes dialogue with the subjects of these complex experiences, since these, in the final analysis, are those responsible for making moral decisions regarding their relationship with God.[17]

HV, now forty years old, thus presents the challenge of how the word of God can shed light on ethical discernment in such complex and involving matters. It represented a courageous initiative in the face of problems that still persist today. For the sake of the very coherence of its service to the gospel, however, it requires a progressive updating, through which its contents and methods might draw closer to the people it set out to help.

Translated by Paul Burns

Notes

1. See, *e.g.*, the growth in bibliography in its first ten years: F.-X. Elizari, 'A los diez años de *Humanae Vitae* – Boletín bibliográfico', *Moralia* 001, 002 (1979), 235–53.

2. In Brazil, the 143-page text from the Fraternity Campaign in 2008 does not quote HV directly, though it does deal with subjects directly linked to human fertility. See CNBB, *Fraternidade e Defesa da Vida Humana*, Brasilia: Campagna da Fraternidade, 2008.
3. J. Gafo, 'La anticoncepción en el Sínodo. Claroscuros del valor profético de la *Humanae Vitae*', *Sal Terrae* 69, 1 (1981), 30.
4. CELAM General Secretariat, *Globalización y Nueva Evangelización*. Reflexiones del CELAM (1999–2003), Bogotá, 2003, p. 25.
5. Figures from IBGE, the Brazilian Institute of Geography and Statistics, Rio de Janeiro, 1994.
6. On the natural law aspect, see E. Borgman, 'Unfixing Nature', in this issue, pp. 73–82 above; also D. Mieth, immediately above.
7. John Paul II, *Veritatis Splendor*. Encyclical Letter, Vatican City: Libreria Editrice Vaticana, 1993.
8. See, *e.g.*, J. Desclos, *Resplendir de vraie liberté*, Montreal: Médiaspaul, 1994.
9. J. Snoek, '*Humanae Vitae*: vinte anos depois', *Perspectiva Teológica* 2 (1998), 310.
10. *Folha de São Paulo*, 16 Apr. 1995, part 1, p. 9.
11. http://espresso.repubblica.it/dettalio-archivio/1464314, accessed 3 Oct. 2007.
12. L. Robeiro, *Sexualidade e reprodução. O que os padres dizen e deixam de dizer*, Petrópolis: Vozes, 2002. pp. 56ff.
13. A. Flávio de Oliveira Pierucci, *Igreja: contradições e acomodação. Ideologia do clero católico sobre a reprodução humana no Brasil*, São Paulo: Ed. Brasilense, 1978, p. 33.
14. L. Ribeiro, *op. cit.*, p. 47.
15. Gaudium et Spes, n. 51.
16. Among the ample bibliography available se the synthesis by V. Peinado, *Eticas teológicas ayer y hoy*, Madrid: San Pablo, 1993.
17. GS, n. 50.

(C) A Philippine Assessment

JOSÉ M. DE MESA

1. Response of the Philippine bishops: initial and eventual

When *Humanae Vitae* was promulgated in July 1968, the Catholic Bishops' Conference of the Philippines (CBCP) quickly, wholeheartedly, and clearly endorsed Pope Paul VI's encyclical the following October.[1] The tenor of their document was one of humble obedience 'to right moral guidance.'[2] In their view disobedience, despite explicit admission on the part of ecclesiastical authorities that it was a non-fallible teaching,[3] could not be countenanced in this predominantly Catholic country on the grounds of conscience. The bishops argued that the pope 'has the charism of the assistance of the Holy Spirit . . . which I do not enjoy in my private studies.'[4] To the Philippine bishops, who today remain influential as a body, the basic reason for any opposition arose from a misunderstanding of Vatican II and one which could be regarded as a 'post-conciliar apostasy presented under the guise of renewal.'[5] This stand had led the institutional Church consistently to oppose, then and now, any attempt by the Philippine government to regulate population growth by promoting modern means of birth control.

To date the official stance of CBCP has remained unchanged. One needs only to consult the most recent authoritative document of the Philippine Church, the *Acts and Decrees of the Second Plenary Council* of 1991 (PCP II), to verify this. Though its tone is less critical than their response in 1968, it nevertheless reiterates firmly and clearly that initial stand: 'The Church, faithful to her teachings, should call on the responsibility of all concerned to help present the notion of responsible Christian parenthood as contained in *Gaudium et Spes, Humanae Vitae,* and *Familiaris Consortio.* In this sense, 'a broader, more decisive and more systematic effort should be undertaken to make the natural methods of regulating fertility known, respected and applied.'[6] It continues to hold 'directly-willed abortion, sterilization and contraception as wrong in themselves.'[7] Consequent to this stand, whenever the government attempts to promote all the available means of regulating births in the face of rapid population growth, the bishops or some representative are quick to reaffirm the official church position of prohibiting contraceptive methods save those that are deemed natural such as rhythm or the ovulation method. It is, of course, curious that official church documents that oppose the artificial means of birth regulation but advocate so-called natural ones do not cite nor even hint at St Augustine's strong condemnation of what may be similar to the rhythm or ovulation methods.[8] One wonders what this silence means.

2. Developments

There has been no real discussion on this subject within the Philippine Church, nor has it been encouraged at any time.[9] However, one comes across occasional advocacy of what the government wants to promote and the rebuttal of this position by the church authorities or church-approved organizations promoting the official ecclesiastical position in family life programmes. The lone Filipina member of the commission set up by Paul VI to advise him on the issue, a demographer, aware of the large number of women utilizing contraception in the country, regards the hard opposition of the Church to all forms of birth regulation in the country as 'unenlightened.'[10] Both Church and government, at least officially, recognize today the growing magnitude of the problem of poverty and population growth.[11]

It may be a mistake, however, to think that the there has been no change at all in the thinking of the Philippine bishops. Development is expressed not only through reversal of what had been previously said, but also through speaking about something else related to it. It is not irrelevant to mention at this juncture the fact that Asian cultures in general and the Filipino culture in particular are high-context cultures.[12] In such cultures there are certain things that need no saying to be communicated. Hence, sensitivity to the context in these cultures is necessary to 'hear' what may not be said explicitly. In contrast, low-context cultures require explicitation of everything that needs to be communicated. It is, therefore, possible to sense a transformation in the bishops' attitude toward marital intercourse when viewed in the light of other declarations they have made. For even if the bishops have explicitly maintained the official church position on this matter of birth regulation, they have recently reflected more deeply on other matters deemed at least equally important, if not more so. In a cultural context where explicit contradiction disrupts harmony and may likely be construed as disrespectful, such a move may be worth noting.

For instance, taking its cue most probably from *Humanae Vitae* itself, the Philippine church leadership had more recently incorporated and even developed the personalist dimension of marriage. Thus, PCP II could state that 'it is the task of the Christian family to reveal and communicate the love of God' by 'forming a community of persons' and 'serving life through procreation and education of offspring.'[13] And if, to take another example, the bishops had sort of pre-empted any possible objection to the encyclical by calling for humble unquestioning obedience in the late 1960s, in the early 1990s they were emphasizing co-responsibility of the laity in a participatory Church, an important aspect of the Church as communion. They declare that the laity cannot be reduced 'to being mere objects of pastoral care, passive and compliant recipients of the clergy's evangelizing effort.'[14] In encouraging the laity to active sharing of responsibility within the Church, the bishops are now wont to say that 'nobody is so poor as to have nothing to give, and nobody is so rich as to have nothing to receive.'[15] Surely, insight from experience would not be excluded in such a contribution.

In this connection one can only welcome the growing positive attitude of the Federation of Asian Bishops' Conferences (FABC), of which the Philippine bishops are part, toward committed marital sexuality expressed in their document on the family during the eighth Plenary Assembly in 2004.[16] Still speaking along the lines of communion, this episcopal body, which had been formed in the late 1970s, asserts that in marital spirituality the total person of wife and husband is involved in the relationship, 'emotions, feelings, the heart and body.' Then it openly breaks away from the mentality that regards sex as suspect and embraces the mutually self-giving conjugal act as 'truly a wondrous gift and mystery from God.'

It describes marital intercourse in an unambiguously positive manner and in a very intimate fashion: 'The profound sense of oneness that married couples experience in the conjugal act, the deep feeling of self-giving love for the beloved, points to *a conjugal mystical experience* where one loses oneself completely for the other. They are drawn to and by the goodness of life and are led to comprehend more profoundly God's very nature as Self-Giving Love (*agape*).' The statement then concludes that 'rather than weakening spirituality as in a dualistic perspective that denigrates the human body, the loving communion of mind and heart expressed in the conjugal act vivifies, supports and strengthens marital spirituality as a spirituality of communion.' This development is significant when one thinks of the suspicion of many that *Humanae Vitae* appeared to have failed to shake off its distrust of sex.[17]

3. Reflection

Theologically, the importance of regarding experience as constitutive in understanding the faith cannot be gainsaid. *Gaudium et Spes* itself follows this pattern of looking at both the gospel and human experience to throw light on particular life situations (cf. G.S. 46). Disregarding experience easily leads to raising wrong questions regarding a specific matter. The formulation of questions is decisive for what will be discussed and how. It seems to my wife and me that the questions raised and answers given by *Humanae Vitae* are not the most important questions for married people. Rather, it is the connection between the marital and familial life and the gospel, and the dichotomy between them, which constitutes 'one of the more serious errors of our age' (G.S. 43). It is, therefore, the *total* good of our marriage and family that was and is the theological-moral framework of our relationship with each other and ours toward our children, not the preoccupation with every sexual act being open to procreation. That it was mainly celibates who were asking the questions is not an unimportant element in the discussion.

One specific element my wife and I sorely miss as a couple in most of the discussions about sex, including of *Humanae Vitae*, is the joy of loving and being married as well as the joy of engaging in sexual intercourse as an expression of committed love.[18] We suspect that it is the continuing distrust of sex brought about by dualism that makes church leadership balk at the delight married couples take in playful sexual passion and bodily enjoyment.[19] This influence may still be behind the declaration of *renouncing* marriage by those who take on a celibate way of life. After all, those who marry do not state that they renounce celibacy! Faced with the unambiguous description of delightful sexual passion of man and woman for each other described in the *Song of Songs* (5.10–16; 7.1–9), the inclination of those in celibate leadership may be to refer to Augustine, who thinks that a man who is too ardent a lover of his wife is an adulterer.[20] But such genuine sexual enjoyment we consider a real compliment to the God who gave us our male and female bodies and who designed them so. For us relishing its goodness is doxological. And this cannot be equated with wanton seeking of pleasure with utter disregard for consequences (hedonism) or with a selfish refusal to have children (egoism) that would lead to moral ruin, which Paul VI's fear-laden encyclical associated it with.[21]

Regarding the particular issue of having children, we think it is worth keeping in mind that marriage is a faith response to the one and only vocation for all Christians: to seek above all the Kingdom of God (Matt. 6.33). Marriage is Christian discipleship. In the decisions that couples make as to how to arrange their life together, how to use money, how to spend time, how to raise children, for instance, they are making religious decisions for or against the Kingdom, which they seek above all in and through their marriage and family life. Likewise, their engaging in sexual intercourse to express and embody their committed love for one another and commitment to what is life-giving is an expression of fidelity or faithfulness to the imperatives of the Kingdom. Against the background of calls for obedience to what *Humanae Vitae* stipulates, it is worth considering what Vatican II says regarding the right to religious freedom and to see how it applies within the Church (cf. *Dignitatis Humanae*, art. 2). Living the marital partnership and making decisions for its total wellbeing are moral imperatives. In these decisions of faith, the freedom of married couples needs rather to be upheld and not coerced in any way.

Undoubtedly, discerning the will of God is part of the Judeo-Christian tradition. We need to consider thoughtfully what it is that God requires of us in the actual circumstances of our lives. But a neglected side of this same tradition is the truth that God has entrusted life to us and what becomes of it (cf. Gen. 1.28),[22] putting into the hands of humanity the responsibility and privilege to make wise decisions about life. We know how empowering trust is. Being trusted instills both confidence and a real sense of responsibility. God is imaged as a trusting God. God has faith in us. This is the Davidic view of living in the context of the Covenant.[23] Life as entrusted to us is, as it were, a blank cheque on which we write out our lives as humanity. One wonders what image of God predominates in *Humanae Vitae* and in the pronouncements that reiterate its stand. Certainly not a God trustful of human beings, confident that ultimately married couples will decide wisely. But, perhaps, a Lawgiver-Judge Deity who promulgates rules, who sees to it that these are followed, and who dispenses a reward-punishment sort of justice.

Finally, as authority was an issue in the publication of *Humanae Vitae* and remains so, mutuality of responsibility arising from Baptism needs a hearing. Adult married Christians are not like children in the Church who are ignorant and, therefore, need to be simply told and led. In a juridically-construed ecclesiology, an active teaching clergy and a passive taught laity was the norm. But with the retrieval of genuine equality in dignity and responsibility by virtue of Baptism in Vatican II (cf. LG 31), the mutual learning and teaching of clergy and laity alike need to be fostered. This belief in mutuality of dignity and responsibility (co-responsibility), which was so enshrined in Vatican II, could have been affirmed and exemplified in *Humanae Vitae* if only Paul VI had taken seriously the experience of married couples as constitutive in understanding the imperatives of the Christian faith – as did the Commission he convened. We know now that it was a missed opportunity.

Notes

1. Catholic Bishops' Conference of the Philippines, 'Pastoral Letter on the Encyclical *Humanae Vitae*,' in Richard P. Hardy, ed., *The Philippine Bishops Speak (1968–1983)*, Quezon City: Maryhill School of Theology, 1984. Hereinafter referred to as CBCP, 'Pastoral Letter.' See also William Shannon, *The Lively Debate*, New York: Sheed & Ward, 1970, pp. 134–5.
2. CBCP, 'Pastoral Letter,' p. 6.
3. CBCP, 'Pastoral Letter,' pp. 10, 14. Cf. Shannon, *The Lively Debate*, p. 114.
4. CBCB, 'Pastoral Letter,' p. 14. See also Shannon, *The Lively Debate*, p. 134. Shannon reports that in Asia the bishops of Sri Lanka called for 'full and loyal assent' of Catholics to the encyclical and the bishops of India pledged their support for it. Similarly, the Japanese bishops called for an obedient reception of the encyclical. *Op. cit.*, pp. 122, 132, 138.
5. CBCP, 'Pastoral Letter,' p. 17. Cf. Shannon, p.135.
6. *Acts and Decrees of the Second Plenary Council of the Philippines*, Manila: CBCP, 1992, p. 242. PCP II was an official council of the Philippine Church participated in by laity, religious, and clergy under the leadership of the CBCP.
7. *Ibid.*, p. 198.
8. See Georg Denzler, *Die verbotene Lust. 2000 Jahre christliche Sexualmoral*, Munich: Piper, 1991, pp. 150–64; Uta Ranke-Heinemann, *Eunuchs for the Kingdom of Heaven: Women, Sexuality, and the Catholic Church*, New York: Doubleday, 1990, pp. 82–4.
9. In the cited pastoral letter, the CBCP states, 'We are happy to note that among our Clergy and leaders of the lay apostolate, not one voice was raised in public against the Encyclical.' CBCP, 'Pastoral Letter,' p. 14.
10. As cited in Robert McClory, *Turning Point*, New York: Crossroad, 1995, p. 161.
11. It is interesting to note that PCP II speaks more about the cultural, social, eco-

nomic, and political problems of the country, particularly the disparity between the rich and the poor, and merely mentions rather than elaborates on the problem of birth control. *Acts and Decrees*, pp. 10–13, 198, 242.
12. Melba Maggay, *Understanding Ambiguity in Filipino Communication Patterns*, Quezon City: Institute for Studies in Asian Church and Culture, 1999, pp. 12–13.
13. *Acts and Decrees*, p. 195.
14. *Ibid.*, p. 39.
15. *Ibid.*, p. 39.
16. Quotations are from Federation of Asian Bishops' Conferences, 'The Asian Family: Toward A Culture of Life' 2004, #104. Emphasis mine. The document was accessed on 29 Sept. 2007 at <http://www.fabc.org/asian_mission_congress/docs/AsianFamily.doc>
17. See *A Lively Debate*, p. 190.
18. A point mentioned by Colette Potvin, a married lay woman in the Papal commission and signer of the majority report, as a 'gift of pleasure and of physical and psychological fulfillment.' See McClory, *Turning Point*, p. 106.
19. Particularly article 17 of *Humanae Vitae*: see McClory, *Turning Point*, p. 116.
20. Cf. Ranke-Heinemann, *Eunuchs for the Kingdom of Heaven*, p. 94.
21. Shannon, *The Lively Debate*, pp. 110–11.
22. A thought reflected in the Majority Report of the Papal Commission set up by Paul VI. McClory, *Turning Point*, pp. 112–14, 172–9.
23. 'What God does first and best and most is to *trust his [people] with their moment of history*. He trusts them, sets them free from the need to please by law, cult or piety. He trusts his [people] not to bring death but to do what must be done for the sake of his whole community.' Walter Brueggeman, *In Man We Trust: The Neglected Side of Biblical Faith*, Atlanta: John Knox Press, 1972, pp. 33–4.

Committed Love and Relational Justice

MARY E. HUNT

Committed love comes in many forms. It is not a 'stage of life' but a grace-filled experience that often, though by no means always, results in the formation of family or community. In Christian life, it forms part of the fabric of the whole community, making it not simply a private matter but part of the common good.

Committed love has previously been sacramentalized and/or legalized in marriage. As cultures increasingly recognize that heterosexual pair-bonding is but one form of committed love, it is time to think critically about additional ways that Christian communities can encourage people to deepen in and sustain such love. Otherwise, both the religious support for and celebration of love is lost for many people with a net loss for the whole community.

Same-sex marriage is the most obvious and disputed contemporary effort to broaden the base of committed love beyond the limits that most societies set. Heterosexism is the limiting of licit love to a woman and a man, and the privileging of that form of love over all others.[1] This form of oppression conditions most Christian Churches' reluctance to embrace same-sex marriage despite the fact that many (though not all) lesbian/gay and bisexual people would be quite content to be married just like their heterosexual counterparts.[2] Efforts to bring about same-sex marriage (successful in countries including Belgium, Canada, the Netherlands, South Africa, Spain, and, in the U.S., the Commonwealth of Massachusetts) have occasioned creative thinking about the nature and variety of committed love that has important implications for Christian Churches.

While marriage seems the obvious locus of discussion, I observe that beginning with it results not in an increase of committed love but an increase of legal contracts. The history of marriage makes clear that the institution has changed continually over millennia but that it has typically involved some form of property exchange and/or sharing that is sanctioned by the state and/or by a religion.[3] As a social contract, marriage is sufficiently elastic to incorporate same-sex couples. But doing so will not necessarily encourage committed love in forms other than dyads. It will, however, level the legal playing field for those in coupled relationships, whether or not they have children, as long as they wish to enter into the rights and responsibilities the legal systems offers. But to build a sacramental dimension in conjunction with this legal one seems to me limited if the goal is to encourage the wide range of ways people experience and express committed love.

Opposition to extending marriage to same-sex couples can be virulent. For example, religious conservatives in the United States, including most Catholic bishops, have made preventing legal recognition of same-sex marriage a high priority. But in this fray one is bound to favour or oppose marriage as if there were no other option for right relationship between and among committed people. That is simply untrue and unhelpful if from a Christian perspective the goal is to enhance and encourage the many forms of committed love that grace this world.

I suggest that relational justice is at stake, not more marriages.[4] While I agree that any couple of legal age and capable of consent should be able to marry, and to divorce for that matter, I want to explore other forms of committed love that beg legal and religious attention. I join movements like Beyondmarriage.org that seek 'a new strategic vision for all our families and relationships.'[5] Extending marriage rights to same-sex couples, while an act of justice in itself, does not address so many other positive forms of human commitment. Indeed it continues to favour one model at the expense of others. Moreover, when criteria for marriage are quantitative (two persons) rather than qualitative (are there children or other persons needing care involved?), I fear that too many people fall through the cracks.

There are many forms of committed love: for example, single parents with children; religious communities; children caring for adult, usually elderly, parents; groups of friends who covenant with one another; not to mention the complexities of polyamorous unions. It would be ethically and theo-politically easy to write all of these off as morally anomalous, not fitting the paradigm of committed love called 'marriage', and move on. Ironically, such a move would virtually require that same-sex love be seen as worthy of marriage since by comparison with these options it differs minimally from the current norm. But a more ambitious effort to rethink committed love and relational justice is in order. The following reflections are a Catholic feminist contribution.

Post-modern life with its rapid tech-driven pace and its globalized context is not terribly conducive to committed love. I consider that a regrettable loss, since love over time is a socially enhancing component of a sometimes isolating and alienating society. Major social factors like wars, borders and immigration restrictions, economic injustice, and the like keep many intimate partners and/or family members apart. Media-fuelled psychological factors including the cult of the young and shapely, the temptation of early, easy sex, and the allure of many partners all discourage long term relationships. New is better not just for cars and mobile phones but for partners. Sex education and reproductive health services have not kept pace with changing mores. As usual, women bear a disproportionate share of the results, including their children. Simply allowing lesbian and gay couples to marry will do little or nothing to change that.

What will help is a renewed focus on human life as essentially relational on a planet that struggles to sustain it. Such an ecofeminist anthropology situates the Christian ethical task in the macro realm rather than peering under a relational microscope to see who is pair bonded with whom. It invites a large-scale re-thinking of what we refer to casually as 'the whole human family'. If indeed we are one family, and one with the animals and the rest of creation, then the choices we make about specific love relationships can be many and varied, more a reflection of divine grace than human conformity. But relational justice is required to connect those individual choices with the well being of the whole community, as well as to see that laws and social programmes include everyone regardless of marital status.

How would religious groups celebrate, indeed in the Catholic sense sacramentalize, that is, lift to public expression, the many forms of committed love? The marriage case is easy with same- and opposite-sex ceremonies differing little if at all. But the challenge is to recognize other forms as equally valid, licit, important, and sacred. For example, religious communities function as places where the committed love of members for one another can be lived out. Contrary to the long tradition of claiming that religious profession is *not* a sacrament, it is time to think just what it is. Obviously it is a form of committed love that involves a number of people who make common choices about their collective life. This needs to be seen for what it is and recognized on an equal level with marriage, i.e., as sacramental.

Another variety that needs attention is that of single people, usually women but also some men, who raise children. While there is no marriage in these cases, there is surely committed love between parent and child that is fraught with responsibilities and in need of communal support. It is time to develop blessing ceremonies and other affirmations that will signal a community's support for such a generous choice. The sacrament of parent-child love remains to be fleshed out.

Still another form of committed love is the relationship of care-giver to care-receiver, often child to adult parent. I know of virtually no structured supports for such an arrangement and many obstacles to it that can be traced to the hegemony of marriage. For example, in countries where health insurance is tied to marriage (as opposed to countries where health care is provided more justly on the basis of being part of the community), getting benefits for someone to whom one is not married proves to be impossible. While religious groups cannot be held responsible for social ills, neither are they blameless when their theology encourages such exclusivist thinking. It is time to celebrate these loving relationships long before they end, not simply at a funeral but along the way.

Yet another way that committed love is lived out is among friends who have no legal or kinship ties, perhaps no sexual connection, but an affective bond. Their sharing of daily life including a welcoming home, a common chequebook from which they are generous donors, and care for one another has no name since they happen to be three instead of two people. How does a Christian community bless and affirm their good lives, lift them up as public witnesses of grace? It is a challenge to imagine since most people are so conditioned to see love in twosomes, but it is real and can be as mysteriously good as any other form of love. By not doing so the community misses an opportunity to affirm committed love. However unintentionally, it gives permission to the larger society to discriminate in favour of those who are married when it comes to legal and financial matters. A new celebration of committed love is needed here.

There are many other forms of committed love to explore. Most of them involve people who are usually thought of as 'single,' a term that is meaningful only if friendship is ignored and/or if pair bonding is normative. Indeed such definitions and the legal and religious actions that result from them contribute to injustices toward those who are not lucky in love or who choose for reasons of their own to live in a more solitary way. Some of our best mystics and/or uncles fall in this category. They prove why same-sex marriage, though obviously a move toward justice if anyone is to marry, is at best a very partial solution to a much more differentiated problem of human variety.

The history of marriage shows the intertwined nature of its religious and civil aspects. So, too, are there religious and civil components to the extension of relational justice to those who do not choose an opposite-sex pair-bonded way of living. A sacramental tradition like Catholicism can be helpful by imagining and experimenting with a variety of rituals that celebrate the goodness of committed love in its myriad forms and, by doing so, encourage it to flourish.

Notes

1. See Patricia Beattie Jung and Ralph F. Smith, *Heterosexism: An Ethical Challenge*, Albany, NY: SUNY Press, 1994, and Marvin M. Ellison and Judith Plaskow (eds), *Heterosexism in Contemporary World Religion: Problem and Prospect*, Cleveland: Pilgrim Press, 2007.
2. Persuasive Catholic arguments in favour of same-sex marriage include Daniel C. Maguire, 'A Catholic Defense of Same-Sex Marriage,' Milwaukee, Wisconsin: Religious Consultation on Population, Reproductive Health and Ethics, 2006, and Patricia Beattie Jung, 'The Call to Wed: Why Catholics Should Celebrate Same-Sex Marriage,' http://www.dignityusa.org/pdf/CallToWed-PBJ.pdf, accessed July 1, 2007.
3. See Marvin Ellison, *Same Sex Marriage: A Christian Ethical Analysis*. Cleveland: Pilgrim Press, 2004, and Rosemary Radford Ruether, *Christianity and the Making of the Modern Family*, Boston: Beacon Press, 2001.
4. See ' Roundtable Discussion: Same-Sex Marriage,' *Journal of Feminist Studies in Religion*, Vol. 21, No. 1, 2005, pp. 83–117 including my introductory piece, 'Same-Sex Marriage and Relational Justice,' pp. 83–92.
5. www.beyondmarriage.org, accessed July 2, 2007.

Contributors

JAMES ALISON was born in 1959 and is a Catholic priest, theologian, and author. He holds a doctorate from the Jesuit theological faculty in Belo Horizonte, Brazil. He teaches, writes, and leads retreats in Europe and North and South America. He is one of the theological exponents of the thought of René Girard, and his books include *The Joy of Being Wrong*, *Faith beyond Resentment: fragments catholic and gay*, and most recently *Undergoing God*. His e-mail address below is currently his most fixed address, and further material of his can be found on www.jamesalison.co.uk.

E-mail: cgfragments@btinternet.com

MARCELLA ALTHAUS-REID holds the Chair of Contextual Theology at the School of Divinity, the University of Edinburgh, Scotland. Originally from Argentina, she has pioneered the area of liberation theology and Queer Studies and published extensively in the area. Her many books include *Indecent Theology: Theological Perversions in Sex, Gender and Politics* (Spanish trans. 2005); *The Queer God* (2004); *Liberation Theology and Sexuality* (2006).

Address: School of Divinity, University of Edinburgh, Edinburgh EH1 2LX, Scotland
E-mail: Marcella.Althaus-Reid@ed.ac.uk

ERIK BORGMAN was born in Amsterdam in 1957. He is Professor of Systematic Theology – Theology of Religion, especially Christianity – in the Department of Religious Studies and Theology of Tilburg University, The Netherlands. He is married with two daughters and is a Lay Dominican. Borgman studied philosophy and theology at the University of Nijmegen. He wrote a dissertation on the different forms of Liberation

Theology and their relation to academic Western theology (1990). Between 1998 and 2004 he worked for the Dutch Province of the Order of Preachers to study and keep alive the theology of Edward Schillebeeckx. He published *Edward Schillebeeckx: a Theologian in his History. Vol. I: A Catholic Theology of Culture* (2003). Between 2000 and 2007 he worked at the interdisciplinary Heyendaal Institute for theology, sciences, and culture at Radboud University in Nijmegen, from 2004 as its academic director. He publishes extensively on the relation between theology, religion, the Christian tradition, and contemporary culture. He is a member of the Board of Directors and the Presidential Board of Concilium.

E-mail: E.P.N.M.Borgman@uvt.nl

JULIE CLAGUE is Deputy Head of the Department of Theology and Religious Studies at the University of Glasgow, where she teaches Christian theology and ethics. She is co-editor of the journal *Political Theology* and a member of the steering committee of the Ecclesiological Investigations Program Unit of the American Academy of Religion. Julie has published widely in the areas of moral theology, Catholic social thought, and bioethics. Most recently she has worked on the question of Catholic tradition and doctrinal change. She is co-editor (with Bernard Hoose and Gerard Mannion) of *Moral Theology for the Twenty-First Century* (2008).

E-mail: J.Clague@arts.gla.ac.uk

PHILIP CULBERTSON is an American-born theologian who has taught at the University of Auckland for the past fifteen years. He is also an ordained Episcopal priest. His current research projects have in various ways involved him deeply in the Pasifika community, and most recently, he is the co-editor of *Penina Uliuli: Contemporary Challenges in Mental Health for Pacific People* (University of Hawaii Press, 2007).

E-mail p.culbertson@auckland.ac.nz.

MÁRCIO FABRI DOS ANJOS holds a doctorate in theology and works as a teacher and researcher at the San Camilo University Centre in São Paulo in Brazil, specializing in theological ethics. He is a member of the Brazilian Society for Bioethics and of the bioethics department of the Medical Council of the

State of São Paulo. The author of numerous articles and chapters in collective works, he has edited *Bioética no Brasil: tendências e perspectives* (2007) and *Vida Religiosa e Novas Gerações: memória, poder e utopia* (2007). Recent articles include 'Para compreender a Espiritualidade em bioética' in *O Mundo do Saúde* 31, 2 (2007); 'Das Brot als Zeichen des Teilens und ses Widerspruchs. Ein ethisch-theologischer Versung' in *Theologisch-Practische Quartalschrift* 155, 1 (2007).

Address: Rua Oliveira Alves 164, 04210-060 São Paulo-SP, Brazil
E-mail: mfabri@terra.com.br

DERYN GUEST lectures in the area of biblical hermeneutics at the University of Birmingham. She is the author of *When Deborah Met Jael: Lesbian Biblical Hermeneutics*, and the co-editor of the *Queer Bible Commentary*. Previously, she worked as a Salvation Army officer and retains a keen interest in the relationship between academia and the practice of religious life, particularly in the ways that this affects those who identify as lesbian, gay, bisexual, or transgender.

Address: Department of Theology, University of Birmingham, Edgbaston, Birmingham B15 2TT, United Kingdom

MARY E. HUNT, Ph.D., is a feminist theologian who is co-founder and co-director of the Women's Alliance for Theology, Ethics and Ritual (WATER) in Silver Spring, Maryland, USA. A Catholic active in the women-church movement, she lectures and writes on theology and ethics with particular attention to liberation issues. She is the editor of *A Guide for Women in Religion: Making Your Way from A to Z* (2004) and co-editor of *Good Sex: Feminist Perspectives from the World's Religions* (2001). Her current project is on heterosexism.

E-mail: mhunt@hers.com

TAVITA MALIKO is a Samoan theological student currently studying for his PhD at the University of Auckland. His current research is in the area of body theology, specifically male body theology. He is also an ordained minister of the Congregational Christian Church of Samoa. He has published one article in the book *Penina Uliuli: Contemporary Challenges in Mental Health for Pacific People* (University of Hawaii Press, 2007).

E-mail: tsmaliko@xtra.co.nz

JOSÉ M. DE MESA is a married Filipino lay theologian. He is a University Fellow at De La Salle University-Manila and Professor of Applied Systematic Theology at the Inter-Congregational Theological Centre in Quezon City, Philippines, as well as currently the Visiting Luzbetak Professor of Gospel and Culture at the Catholic Theological Union in Chicago. He holds an M.A. and Ph.D. in Religious Studies from the Katholieke Universiteit Leuven in Belgium. Among his main publications are *In Solidarity with the Culture* and *Marriage is Discipleship*, and he has recently published *Why Theology is Never Far Away from Home, Mga Aral sa Daan*, and *The Prayer Our Lord Taught Us*.

E-mail: kajosedemesa@yahoo.com

DIETMAR MIETH was born in 1940 and studied theology, German culture, and philosophy in Freiburg, Trier, Munich, and Wurzburg. From 1974 to 1981 he was Professor of Moral Theology at the university of Fribourg, then Professor of Theological Ethics at the Catholic Theological Faculty of Tübingen, where since 1986 he has led the inter-faculty Centre for Ethics in Science. He was a member of the Advisory Group for Ethics of the E.U. Commission from 1994 to 2000 and has since advised the German Parliament on 'Ethics and Rights in Modern Medicine'. His more recent publications include *Meister Eckhart. Einheit mit Gott* (2002); *Patente und Leben* (jpoint ed., 2003); *Kleine Ethikschule* (2004); *Bioethics in Cultural Contexts: Reflections on Methods and Finitude* (joint ed., 2006); *Ethik – Geschlecht – Wissenschaft (joint ed., 2006)*.

E-mail: dietmar.mieth@uni-tuebingen.de

CHARLES P. RYAN is an Irish priest member of St Patrick's Missionary Society. He studied moral theology at the Academia Alfonsiana, Rome, and at other universities in Ireland and Rome. Since 1968 he has taught at various third-level institutions in Ireland, USA, and Nigeria (for twenty-eight years) and is currently head of Moral Theology in St Joseph's Theological Institute, Cedara, South Africa. He has published articles and chapters on various aspects of moral theology.

Address: P.O.Box 5000, Hilton 3245, South Africa.
E-mail: cpryan@mweb.co.za

NORBERT RECK was born in 1961. He holds a Doctorate in theology, teaches theology and philosophy at the Katholische Stiftungsfachhochschule (Catholic University of Applied Sciences) in Munich and edits the German version of *Concilium*. His 1998 doctoral thesis was on the significance for theology of the testimonies of victims of the German concentration camps in the Nazi era. He also writes for radio and is a consultant in religious education. His publications include: *Im Angesicht der Zeugen. Eine Theologie nach Auschwitz* (1998); *Abenteuer Gott. Den christlichen Glauben neu denken* (2003); *Mit Blick auf die Täter. Fragen an die Theologie nach 1945* (with B. Krondorfer and K. von Kellenbach; 2006).

Address: Arndtstrasse 5, D-80469 Munich, Germany.
E-Mail: norbert.reck@mnet-mail.de.

FELIX WILFRED, born in India in 1948, studied in Rome and Perugia in Italy and in Caen in France. He holds a Master's Degree in Philosophy and a Doctorate in Theology. A Catholic priest, he is President of the Faculty of Arts, Chairperson of the School of Philosophy and Religious Thought, and Head of Department of Christian Studies at the State University of Madras in India. His latest books include *Margins: The Site of Asian Theologies* (2007); *Dalit Empowerment* (^{2}2007); *The Sling of Utopias. Struggles for a Different Society* (2005); *Asian Dreams and Christian Hope – At the Dawn of the Millennium*, (2003; revised ed.); *From the Dusty Soil – Contextual Reinterpretation of Christianity* (1995).

Address: Asian Centre for Cultural and Contextual Studies, 40/6A Pamayur Kuppan Road, Sholinganallur Post, Panayur, Madras 6009, India
E-Mail: Concilium.madras@gmail.com

CONCILIUM
International Review of Theology

FOUNDERS
Anton van den Boogaard; Paul Brand; Yves Congar, OP†; Hans Küng;
Johann Baptist Metz; Karl Rahner, SJ†; Edward Schillebeeckx

BOARD OF DIRECTORS
President
Felix Wilfred

Vice Presidents
Erik Borgman; Diego Irarrázaval; Susan Ross

BOARD OF EDITORS
Regina Ammicht Quinn (Frankfurt, Germany)
Maria Clara Bingemer (Rio de Janeiro, Brazil)
Erik Borgman (Nijmegen, The Netherlands)
Lisa Sowle Cahill (Boston, USA)
Eamonn Conway (Limerick, Ireland)
Dennis Gira (Paris, France)
Hille Hacker (Frankfurt, Germany)
Diego Irarrázaval (Santiago, Chile)
Solange Lefebvre (Montreal, Canada)
Daniel Marguerat (Lausanne, Switzerland)
Éloi Messi Metogo (Yaoundé, Cameroon
Paul D. Murray (Durham, UK)
Susan Ross (Chicago, USA)
Silvia Scatena (Reggio Emilia, Italy)
Jon Sobrino SJ (San Salvador, El Salvador)
Luiz Carlos Susin (Porto Alegre, Brazil)
Andrés Torres Queiruga (Santiago de Compostela, Spain)
Marie-Theres Wacker (Münster, Germany)
Elaine Wainwright (Auckland, New Zealand)
Felix Wilfred (Madras, India)

PUBLISHERS
SCM-Canterbury Press (London, UK)
Matthias-Grünewald Verlag (Ostfildern, Germany)
Editrice Queriniana (Brescia, Italy)
Editorial Verbo Divino (Estella, Spain)
Editora Vozes (Petrópolis, Brazil)

Concilium Secretariat:
Asian Centre for Cross-cultural Studies,
40/6A, Panayur Kuppam Road, Sholinganallur Post, Panayur, Madras 600119, India.
Phone: +91- 44 24530682 Fax: +91- 44 24530443
E-mail: *Concilium.madras@gmail.com*
Managing Secretary: Pramila Rajan

Concilium Subscription Information

February   2009/1: *Heritage*

April   2009/2: *Theology of Creation*

June   2009/3: *God, Monotheism*

October   2009/4: *Fathers of Latin American Theology*

December   2009/5: *Translation of the Bible*

New subscribers: to receive *Concilium 2008* (five issues) anywhere in the world, please copy this form, complete it in block capitals and send it with your payment to the address below.

Please enter my subscription for *Concilium 2008*

Individuals
- ____ £40.00 UK
- ____ £60.00 overseas
- ____ $110.00 North America/Rest of World
- ____ €99.00 Europe

Institutions
- ____ £55.00 UK
- ____ £75.00 overseas
- ____ $140 North America/Rest of World
- ____ €125.00 Europe

Postage included – airmail for overseas subscribers

Payment Details:
Payment must accompany all orders and can be made by cheque or credit card
I enclose a cheque for £/$/€ _____ Payable to SCM-Canterbury Press Ltd
Please charge my Visa/MasterCard (Delete as appropriate) for £/$/€ _____
Credit card number _____
Expiry date _____
Signature of cardholder _____
Name on card _____
Telephone _____ E-mail _____

Send your order to *Concilium*, SCM-Canterbury Press Ltd
13–17 Long Lane, London EC1A 9PN, UK
E-Mail: office@scm-canterburypress.co.uk

Customer service information:
All orders must be prepaid. Subscriptions are entered on an annual basis (i.e. January to December). No refunds on subscriptions will be made after the first issue of the Journal has been despatched. If you have any queries or require information about other payment methods, please contact our Customer Services department.

New from Canterbury Press Norwich

IN SEARCH OF THE LOST

Richard Anthony Carter

In 2003, seven members of the Melanesian Brotherhood, an order of Christian brothers living a simple and prayerful life and known for their peace work throughout the South Pacific and beyond, were kidnapped as a result of ethnic conflict in the Solomon Islands. For four months Christians all over the world hoped and prayed desperately for their release, then came the news that they were already dead, brutally murdered soon after their capture. This extraordinarily powerful and moving account tells the harrowing story of the loss of seven good, young and holy lives and the aftermath of those deaths as a community tries to make sense of violence and tragedy. It recounts the challenge of living the Christian faith when confronted by fear and great loss and the way of redemption and healing.

"One of the most truly evangelical books I have read for a long time"
Archbishop Rowan Williams

ISBN 978-1-85311-780-0
256pp + 8pp plate section
216x135mm   Paperback

£12.99

Available from good bookshops,
or (adding £2.50 per order to cover postage) direct from the publisher

CANTERBURY PRESS NORWICH

St Mary's Works, St Mary's Plain, Norwich NR3 3BH, UK
Telephone: 01603 612914   Fax: 01603 624483
E-mail: orders@scm-canterburypress.co.uk
Web-site: www.scm-canterburypress.co.uk

Visa, Delta, MasterCard and Switch accepted

Please make cheques payable to SCM-Canterbury Press Ltd

ARL078

Canterbury Studies in Spiritual Theology

At a time when the Church faces many challenges, from within its own ranks as well as from the secular world, this Series aims to help clergy and laity alike to think, act and respond to the complexities of the age with greater confidence, by collecting together the writings of outstanding figures who have shaped core Anglican belief, practice and identity.

THE SACRAMENTAL LIFE
Selected writings of Gregory Dix
Edited by Simon Jones

Gregory Dix - Anglican Benedictine monk, scholar, writer and broadcaster - was one of the most engaging public figures of his day. His classic work, *The Shape of Liturgy*, has remained in print for sixty years, and is an unsurpassed account of the origins of the Eucharist. Apart from the *magnum opus*, Gregory Dix left many pamphlets, papers, sermons, radio talks and other unpublished texts. From this remarkable archive, Simon Jones has created a text that will be valued in teaching, study and as devotional reading for a new generation.

978-1-85311-717-6   224pp   234x156mm
Paperback   Published September 2007   **£16.99**

Other titles in the series

GLORY DESCENDING - Michael Ramsey and his writings
Douglas Dales, John Habgood, Geoffrey Rowell and Rowan Williams
One of the most outstanding Christian leaders of the twentieth century left a legacy of remarkable writings
978-1-85311-630-8   Available now   **£18.99**

THE TRUTH-SEEKING HEART - Selected writings of Austin Farrer
Ann Loades and Robert MacSwain
This is the first attempt to bring together in one accessible volume Farrer's most characteristic thoughts
978-1-85311-712-1   Available now   **£16.99**

TO BUILD CHRIST'S KINGDOM - Selected writings of F.D. Maurice
Jeremy Morris
Arguably the most significant Anglican thinker of his age whose influence on contemporary identity is immense
978-1-85311-777-0   Available now   **£16.99**

FIRMLY I BELIEVE - An Oxford Movement reader
Raymond Chapman
The Oxford Movement sprang into life in the 1830s in reaction to increasing Parliamentary control of the Church
978-1-85311-722-0   Available now   **£16.99**

HAPPINESS AND HOLINESS - Selected writings of Thomas Traherne
Denise Inge
This concise introduction to Traherne's life and work places him in an historical and intellectual context
978-1-85311-789-3   Available January 2008   **£16.99**

---

*Available from good bookshops,
or (adding £2.50 per order to cover postage) direct from the publisher*

CANTERBURY PRESS NORWICH

St Mary's Works, St Mary's Plain, Norwich NR3 3BH, UK
Telephone: 01603 612914   Fax: 01603 624483
E-mail: orders@scm-canterburypress.co.uk
Web-site: www.scm-canterburypress.co.uk

Visa, Delta, MasterCard and Switch accepted

Please make cheques payable to SCM-Canterbury Press Ltd

www.ingramcontent.com/pod-product-compliance
Lightning Source LLC
Chambersburg PA
CBHW070643300426
44111CB00013B/2231